"Abby Johnson is a miracle in today's world, as she is *honest*. While many, if not most, hide or even double down after realizing a fatal flaw in what they believe, Abby changed her entire life. She was honest with God and with herself. God transformed her, and with any luck, he may also transform you into a deliverer of *Fierce Mercy*."

Glenn Beck, radio host and television producer

"Abby Johnson defines God's mercy as 'his divine undeserved favor and compassion.' She is so right. Just look around and you'll see a world that is hurting and broken—a world that desperately needs to know unconditional love and limitless compassion. In this book, Abby will challenge you to learn how to intentionally model God's mercy with a fearsome dedication to love broken people. I hope you will accept her challenge. We need *Fierce Mercy* now more than ever."

Janet Parshall, nationally syndicated talk show host

"What do the survivor of a failed abortion attempt and a former abortion clinic manager have in common? More than you can imagine. Reading Abby Johnson's book *Fierce Mercy* left me nodding my head in agreement, time and time again, with lessons learned in life and in ministry and through examples of God's great mercy on each of us and how we're called to live that out accordingly."

Melissa Ohden, founder of the Abortion Survivors Network

"Abby's new book, *Fierce Mercy*, is fire! It is a bold and powerful testimony of how God will take every messy or marvelous moment we give him and use it for his glory. *Fierce Mercy* will challenge you, change you, and inspire you to believe for the unbelievable. Abby's honesty is captivating and refreshing. Her discovery of who she was created to be, through all the painful and hope-filled turns, makes it hard to put this book down. Be prepared to confront inescapable truths and have your heart reignited with an urgency to live out your God-given purpose!"

Ryan & Bethany Bomberger,
cofounders of The Radiance Foundation

"I knew Abby Johnson for eight years before her conversion. Having had a front-row seat during her journey, I know our world needs *Fierce Mercy*. Abortion is the gravest evil of our time, and this must-read book shares the reality that no heart, no soul, is ever lost. Transformation is possible, conversion is possible, salvation is possible. A culture of death can only be conquered by mercy. Read this book and allow God to use you as an instrument of his mercy and love."

Shawn Carney, cofounder, CEO, and president of 40 Days for Life; bestselling author of *The Beginning of the End of Abortion, To the Heart of the Matter,* and *What to Say When: The Complete New Guide to Discussing Abortion*

"Abby Johnson's *Fierce Mercy* is a beautiful book about how to find the extraordinary in the ordinary, how to find hope in the pain, and how God's truth and mercy compel people to change their lives. From the many unbelievable stories Abby shares from the front lines to the authentic and vulnerable mishaps that happened along the way, this book will inspire you to fully recognize, receive, and give God's mercy."

Amy Ford, founder of Embrace Grace, Inc;
author of *Help Her Be Brave*

"Far from giving permission for evil, mercy fiercely destroys it and frees us from its grasp. I have been blessed to see the story of this book firsthand, not only in ministering to Abby but also in ministering to so many like her since 1993. I want to thank her for putting a spotlight on mercy, including how it transformed her, how she has led others to it, and how it is a road map for our movement."

Fr. Frank Pavone, national director of Priests for Life; pastoral director of Rachel's Vineyard and Silent No More

"While the world watched Abby Johnson's exodus from America's abortion empire, Planned Parenthood, little did they know the profound, private journey going on within her own heart and mind as God gifted her with a special assignment. You'll learn not only what happened right after Abby left Planned Parenthood but also how God used her 'yes' to rescue hundreds of abortion workers after her—and just how far, wide, and deep his grace, redemption, and mercy are. Abby shows us how powerfully God can use any one of us to change the world, no matter our story."

Lauren Muzyka, founder, president, and CEO of Sidewalk Advocates for Life

"Abby's story of redemption should give hope to anyone who feels that God's mercy is out of reach in their life. God's mercy is an undeserved gift given out of boundless love, and Abby has responded by telling that story in hopes that it will reach those who need it most. From the personal stories of those who have dedicated their lives to saving the least of these, we can learn a lot about overcoming the defeatist messages of an industry committed to profiting from the deaths of the innocent by lying to their mothers about the help and hope available to them."

Kristan Hawkins, president of Students for Life of America and host of *Explicitly Pro-Life Podcast*

"On the road to Damascus, a zealous persecutor of Christians experienced a profound conversion. Following that conversion, the apostle Paul began his most important work: shaping the church and impacting the world. Similarly, Planned Parenthood director Abby Johnson experienced a profound conversion, as related in the book and movie *Unplanned*. But what followed that conversion has been Abby's most important work: inspiring millions, launching game-changing ministries, galvanizing the pro-life movement, and transforming lives around the world. I've personally witnessed Abby's story unfold and am continually inspired by what God can accomplish through a life radically reoriented to him. Inside these pages, you may even discover how he can use *you* to change the world."

David Bereit, founder of 40 Days for Life

FIERCE
MERCY

FIERCE MERCY

DARING TO LIVE OUT
GOD'S COMPASSION
IN BOLD AND PRACTICAL WAYS

ABBY JOHNSON
WITH CINDY LAMBERT

BakerBooks
a division of Baker Publishing Group
Grand Rapids, Michigan

Published by Baker Books
a division of Baker Publishing Group
PO Box 6287, Grand Rapids, MI 49516-6287
www.bakerbooks.com

Printed in the United States of America

Library of Congress Cataloging-in-Publication Data
Names: Johnson, Abby, author. | Lambert, Cindy, other.
Title: Fierce mercy : daring to live out God's compassion in bold and practical ways / Abby Johnson with Cindy Lambert.
Description: Grand Rapids, MI : Baker Books, a division of Baker Publishing Group, [2022] |
Identifiers: LCCN 2021041268 | ISBN 9781540901576 | ISBN 9781540901996 (casebound) | ISBN 9781493434114 (ebook)
Subjects: LCSH: God (Christianity)—Mercy. | Mercy. | Pro-life movement. | Abortion—Moral and ethical aspects. | Johnson, Abby.
Classification: LCC BT153.M4 J65 2022 | DDC 231/.6—dc23
LC record available at https://lccn.loc.gov/2021041268

Some names and details have been changed to protect the privacy of the individuals involved.

The Author is represented by Ambassador Literary Agency.

Baker Publishing Group publications use paper produced from sustainable forestry practices and post-consumer waste whenever possible.

22   23   24   25   26   27   28   7   6   5   4   3   2   1

To my beautiful children:
Grace, Alex, Luke, Carter, Jude, Lucy, Maggie,
and Fulton. You sacrifice time with your mom
so that other children will live to be with their moms.
Being a mother to each of you has
made my heart whole.

CONTENTS

1

REVEALED

I knew I was in the right place the moment I saw the six-foot-high black-iron fence up ahead. I wasn't surprised to see it. After all, there'd be no authentic filming of the critical scenes of my life without the notorious fence that had served as the dividing line between prolifers and abortion workers during my eight years as the director of a Planned Parenthood center in Bryan, Texas.

I pulled up to a police officer guarding the movie set lot and rolled down the window of my rental car. "I'm Abby Johnson, here as a guest for the filming of *Unplanned*," I said. He moved aside and waved me through.

The flutter of excitement I felt intensified as I cruised the parking lot for an open spot and parked. I'd never been on a movie set before, let alone a movie about *me*. Telling *my* story. I wasn't sure what the day would be like, but I'd been filled with anticipation as I'd flown into Oklahoma City, then driven the ninety minutes to Stillwater, Oklahoma, at the invitation of directors Chuck Konzelman and Cary Solomon.

Approaching the fence on the set brought a flood of memories from my time at Planned Parenthood. Had it really been nearly nine years since I'd resigned as director? The original fence surrounding that center was taken down about four years after my resignation. The center then closed its doors forever, and the building was purchased by 40 Days for Life and transformed into their national headquarters. The last time I drove by 4112 East 29th Street in Bryan, I admired the welcoming landscaping. Pretty shrubbery rather than imposing iron now surrounds the office building where so much death once took place and so much drama once unfolded.

Here on the set, it seemed they weren't filming at the moment, but a number of people were standing around on the sidewalk. I started to weave through them on the way to the directors' tent as Sheila, the cast director, had instructed me. It was then that I heard the whispers.

"That's Abby Johnson."

"Abby Johnson's on the set."

I briefly felt self-conscious, but soon I was getting hugs and warm welcomes, letting me know I was among friends, though I'd never met any of these members of the cast and crew before.

Only a handful of people had known I was coming—Chuck and Cary; Sheila; and Julie, the PR manage. I spotted Chuck and Cary making their way toward me with welcoming smiles. They both gave me a warm hug, then Chuck said, "Come this way. Sit in the tent where the screens are. You'll be able to see the shot being filmed and what it looks like on camera."

As I stepped into the tent, I saw two rows of directors' chairs and two screens. I was introduced to some of the producers. Someone handed me a set of headphones, which they called *cans*, and I heard a voice yell, "Action."

I watched the screens as a scene with the actress playing me began. What a surreal experience to watch "myself" coming out of the abortion facility with "my" baby bump, holding balloons and gift bags. I instantly knew they were filming the day my coworkers threw me a baby shower for my first child, Grace. Extras on the sidewalk were playing the prolifers, and a sidewalk counselor was talking to "me" through the fence.

At first, I felt a thrill. They'd really captured the moment. But as I watched myself on-screen juggling the gift bags and balloons and then struggling to get them all into "my" little red car while talking with the sidewalk counselor, my feelings of excitement and anticipation suddenly melted into discomfort and then embarrassment. My neck started to tingle and grow hot, and I could feel myself blushing as my stomach twisted in knots.

Oh my word. Everyone is going to see the person I was, and that wasn't a good person. They're going to see me at my worst. There I am, thirty-nine weeks pregnant, on an abortion day, no less—a day I spent ushering women into the abortion chamber—lightheartedly leaving a baby shower to celebrate the life inside of me. Everybody is about to see just how inconsistent and despicable my life and beliefs were.

What am I doing? Why am I allowing this film to happen? The worst part of me is about to be revealed to everyone on the planet who watches this movie. Everyone is going to hate me. They're going to think I'm a terrible person, because I was a terrible person.

I felt exposed and utterly vulnerable. Naked. So few people in my life now knew the person I was when I worked at the clinic. Not even my husband, Doug, or my parents really knew, because they never saw how badly I often behaved on that sidewalk toward the prolifers. They never saw the volatile side of Abby.

Cary was sitting next to me and must have noticed my discomfort. He gently reached over and put his hand on mine.

"Cut," someone yelled, and the screens went blank. I realized I must have been holding my breath because I suddenly took a deep breath.

Cary turned and looked at me, and I met his gaze. "Abby," he said, "this is going to save a lot of lives."

And that was exactly what I needed to hear in that moment. It reminded me that this movie wasn't really about me at all. That wasn't the film's purpose. Yeah, the world was going to see the person I was—warts and flaws and inconsistencies all exposed. Whatever! But at the end of the day, this wasn't about what viewers thought of me. Telling my story was about showing the audience how God could transform a heart, the impact one changed person can have on our culture, and the lives that can be saved because of it. It was like the Holy Spirit spoke to me through Cary. And then I was okay. I was more than okay. I was even more committed to God's purpose in exposing my story to the world.

And it's a good thing too, because I immediately discovered that what I had seen was just the first take. I sat there and watched that same scene reenacted over and over again as they did take after take—at least fifteen times. With each take, my understanding of who I used to be—ambitious, misguided, deceptive, egocentric, inconsistent—grew, yet my shame shrunk smaller and smaller as I was reminded of God's immeasurable mercy toward me.

Mercy. God's divine undeserved favor and compassion.

When I left the set that afternoon and headed to a speaking event to share God's mercy with others, I felt renewed in my purpose. I was living proof that God can change hearts. That he redeems despicable lives. That he forgives. That we are precious to him, and he wants to use us to reach out in his mercy toward others.

I couldn't wait to come back to the set to see how God was going to use this movie. Fortunately, I didn't have to wait long.

THE DAY SOON CAME when once again I took my place in a canvas-backed chair and settled in, placing a pair of headphones over my ears. As I looked at the screen this time, I saw Dr. Anthony Levatino, who, in real life, is a former abortionist. How fitting that Chuck and Cary had recruited him to play the abortion doctor in the film. I saw Julie, one of the clients of And Then There Were None, our ministry to former abortion workers. She used to be an abortion nurse. She lives about an hour and a half outside of Stillwater, and during casting she let me know she really wanted to be involved in the movie. I contacted the directors and asked if she could play a part. They said, "How does she feel about playing an abortion nurse since she used to be one?" I couldn't imagine better casting, and Julie felt up to the part.

Seeing Julie and Dr. Levatino on the set together made me realize what scene they were filming—the ultrasound abortion that changed my life.

I felt a little anxious, not knowing what it would be like for me to relive that horrendous moment as it was reenacted before my eyes. It's one thing to talk about it and relive it in your head. It's a different thing to actually watch it play out.

"ACTION!"

I watched "myself" enter the scene, and I could see the back of the ultrasound machine I'd be watching during the abortion. Dr. Levatino and nurse Julie were doing a great job—they set the tone for the room perfectly. Though they had no acting experience, they simply reenacted the real roles they'd played for years. The doctor explained to "Abby" that he preferred ultrasound-guided abortions and asked her to hold the ultrasound wand. Their patient lay on the table, and they began the abortion procedure.

I suddenly realized I was holding my breath, so I took some deep breaths. I really wanted to hold it together. I felt eyes on me. A ministry team was on set every day of filming. Their role was to pray over everything that was going on. Every morning they led a devotional with the cast and crew. Gabriel, one of the men on the prayer team, was watching me with concern on his face. I felt him put his hand on my shoulder. And Joe, who was running sound, was watching me, as was Meagan, my friend and assistant, just a few seats away. My eyes were drawn back to the screen.

There the actress was holding the wand just as I had on that day, watching the ultrasound screen. Of course, the ultrasound screen remained black as the cameras rolled, but the actress performed as if she were watching the abortion take place. I watched her face. It was becoming troubled, then clearly alarmed. Then I saw disgust and horror consume her.

My shock at the real ultrasound images I'd watched on the screen nine years before flooded my memory. I'd never before witnessed what goes on inside the womb during an abortion. First the image of that perfectly formed baby. Then the sight of it being violently twisted until it crumpled, sucked into the cannula until everything was gone. Only nothingness—an empty uterus left behind.

Ashley abruptly rushed out of the room just as I had.

"Cut."

I completely lost it. A shudder ran through me, and I began to sob. Joe immediately came over and wrapped his arms around me. I probably cried for at least five minutes as he held me. Then in a gentle voice he said, "When people see this, they'll never be the same."

Again, it was just what I needed to hear. I was able to stop crying and step back from Joe's kind embrace.

I knew they were going to use a combination of real ultrasound images and CGI to re-create exactly what happens on an ultrasound screen during an abortion so the audience would see the truth for themselves. It was a bold decision by Chuck and Cary, and I supported it 100 percent. While it would be difficult to watch, it was an opportunity to let the horror of abortion speak for itself. I knew beyond a doubt that this scene would save lives. That thought infused me with strength. I knew I would be able to watch the retakes to come.

And so I did. After several retakes, they called a break, so I checked in with Dr. Levatino and Julie to see how they were doing. We comforted each other with assurances of this scene's importance in saving lives. And then they did more retakes.

Dr. Levatino's wife, such a sweet lady, was sitting beside me, and I could tell she was getting a bit emotional. I realized that she was confronting, perhaps for the first time, the person her husband had been and the role he had played in the deaths of so many children—something she hadn't seen for herself before. I put my hand over hers, and she grabbed it. The tension during those takes was visible on all our faces. It seemed to even be in the air.

"Okay. I think we're good. I think we got it," someone called out. I could feel relief wash over the entire set.

I immediately walked over to Dr. Levatino, we hugged, and I said, "Are you okay?"

"I just did that for way too long," he answered, emotional fatigue visible on his face and in his posture.

I then gave Julie a hug and said, "How about you? Are you okay?"

"Yes. I really wish I could say that I had not been that sort of nurse in the room. But that callousness, that is who we were."

"Yes, it was," I admitted.

That's what made it all so painful. We weren't filming a work of fiction. This scene was real. It had happened before my eyes and is still happening in abortion centers all over the world every day.

As I drove away from the set that evening, I thought about the images audiences were going to see on huge movie screens. I knew nobody was going to be able to watch that movie— prolife or pro-choice—and then walk out and say, "Well, I didn't know." Now they would know. If they walked out and said, "Still, I support abortion," at least they clearly knew what they were supporting. They were going to walk out with the truth.

As I write these words, it has been close to a year since the movie *Unplanned* was released in theaters—a movie that helped pull back the curtain on the abortion industry and the reality of abortion. And it has now been ten years since I witnessed the horror of what really happened during the abortion in which I was holding the wand. Ten years since my dramatic conversion. Ten years since I walked out of that Planned Parenthood facility and desperately, clumsily, began following God's lead in becoming an advocate for the un-born. Over those ten years, I've seen God move in so many mighty ways. He has brought the prolife movement so far. But there is so much further to go. So much left to be done! Those who value precious human life can no longer be complacent or dismiss what abortion is and how it hurts our women, our families, and our society.

I've not only seen how far God has brought the prolife movement, but I've also seen how far he has brought me, personally. It's time to tell the story of what has been unfolding these past ten years. Just as I did in the book *Unplanned*, it's time for me to share new chapters of the story God has been writing in my own life. I am seeing what happens when God's truth and mercy compel people to change—change their minds and their hearts. I am on the front lines. I am seeing conversion. I am seeing healing. I am seeing raw, unfiltered mercy at work.

I'm concerned that, for some people, *mercy* may be only a vague theological word. But for me, it's not. Mercy is the powerful, eye-opening force that rushed through me, evoking compassion for the unnamed child on the ultrasound screen that day. Mercy is the flood of relief and peace that later soothed the jagged edges of my tortured, guilt-ridden soul.

From my unique vantage point, I am a witness that God's mercy is on the move. I've developed a passion to fan mercy's flames and multiply its impact. My heart is burning to give testimony to what God's mercy is accomplishing not only on the front lines of the prolife movement but also far beyond that—to wherever believers are responding to the hurt and shame and guilt and pain in our very broken world.

So, mercy is what this book is all about.

And when I say *mercy*, I'm not talking about some wishy-washy, namby-pamby, sentimental, look-the-other-way, wink-at-evil, whitewashing, feel-good self-talk. I'm talking about the tenacious, gritty, powerful, ground-shaking, bone-rattling, life-transforming, soul-invading, life-giving, force-of-God's-power-flooding-every-dark-and-shadowy-nook-and-cranny-of-the-heart kind of mercy.

I'm talking about *fierce* mercy.

Mercy is God's divine, undeserved favor and compassion. *Fierce* means marked by unrestrained zeal, intense, furiously active, and highly determined.

It's time for us all to dive into God's fierce mercy.

To truly recognize it.

To fully receive it.

To generously give it.

When we fully immerse ourselves in God's fierce mercy and commit ourselves to living in it, we dare to do what this world most needs—what is hard, what is right, and what is good. We dare to live out God's compassion in bold and practical ways so that hearts are changed—like mine was.

When God spoke through the prophet Micah in the verse below, he told us in no uncertain terms how important a role mercy is to play in our lives. God wasn't giving us a suggestion or a recommendation to love mercy. He made it a requirement!

I pray that as you read this book, you will leap at this opportunity to explore the life-changing, world-changing power of fierce mercy.

> He has shown you, O mortal, what is good.
> And what does the LORD require of you?
> To act justly and to love mercy
> and to walk humbly with your God.
>
> Micah 6:8

2

VOICES

Mercy is God's love in action. It is not simply a feeling. It is an attribute of God—one that we can reflect and emulate. Look at 1 Peter 1:3 to see what God's mercy prompted him to do. "Praise be to the God and Father of our Lord Jesus Christ! In his great mercy he has given us new birth into a living hope through the resurrection of Jesus Christ from the dead." It was God's mercy that moved him to give us new birth. When we internalize God's mercy, it compels us to act as well.

As I contemplate the role of mercy in my life, I am struck by the observation that each of the major "mercy encounters" I have had with God propelled me to take action. It was as if I literally couldn't sit still. It seems to me that each time, God penetrated my world with his voice in the most unexpected ways to call me into these mercy experiences. By looking back and recognizing these encounters, I've been stirred to look forward with fresh anticipation of how God might speak to me.

The first time in my life I ever cried out for God's mercy came on Friday, October 23, 2009, at ten o'clock at night. Just four weeks earlier, I'd witnessed the ultrasound abortion that forever changed me. In that brief thirty days, I'd left behind my career at Planned Parenthood with no idea of where I was headed, lost all my closest friends, and come face-to-face with a conscience that had apparently been sound asleep most of my adult life. My life had been completely upended. Then one Friday night (while in the shower, of all places), I felt a certain and distinct call from the Lord to immediately go back to my old abortion clinic and pray. I was baffled as to why I was being drawn there but couldn't ignore the inaudible yet compelling voice.

At the fence surrounding the darkened, closed building, I stood and faced my egregious sins for the very first time. It was then that I realized how broken and wretched I truly was. (Until such a realization, we won't recognize that we even need mercy.) As I stood sobbing over this realization, I wasn't alone. There at the fence were two prolifers, praying. Once they learned who I was and why I was at the clinic, they were ecstatic, to say the least, for they knew that in my repentance they were seeing God's merciful answer to the many prayers offered there. So, while they literally danced in thanksgiving, I shuddered with sobs of remorse as tears of relief and gratitude streamed down like rain.

What a picture of mercy! A holy, mysterious blend of a human's contrite humility accompanied by heaven's celebration. Of Good Friday sacrifice blended with Easter Sunday victory. Of intensely private communion between one human soul and the Holy Spirit of the living God broadcast so that all of heaven can look on in rapt awe.

How fitting, then, that my mercy journey hasn't been a whispered experience behind drawn curtains. No. The not-so-private life of Abby Johnson—both the blunders and the healing—has mostly been lived out loud and in public. After all, less than a month after I left the abortion industry, thanks to Planned Parenthood's decision to file a court case against me (which was later dismissed), my face was all over the national news. It was like being shot out of a cannon. And it wasn't at all comfortable! I didn't have time to quietly reflect or prepare or heal or even be alone. Cameras and microphones being shoved in my face came with the territory—ready or not.

I certainly didn't feel ready or qualified to speak on behalf of the prolife movement. After all, I'd been using my voice to fight it for years. But I did feel qualified (and compelled) to share my experience—of God changing my mind because of what I'd seen on that ultrasound screen and of what I'd seen and heard as a clinic director that exposed the truth of Planned Parenthood's goals and objectives. Romans 9:16 says, "It does not, therefore, depend on human desire or effort, but on God's mercy." The events I found myself thrust into were proving to me that it was God's mercy, not my own desires or efforts, that both qualified and compelled me to speak out publicly.

In a heartbeat, I was asked to speak on dozens of national news shows. So, I told my story and answered questions with raw honesty, which led to many prolife groups inviting me to speak.

My first in-person speaking engagement took place in the warm basement of a church in New York City in front of a hundred people. There I discovered that, in the telling of my story, there was healing not only for me but also for those who were listening. Women lined up, often in tears, and told me their abortion stories and secrets.

Soon I was speaking all over the country. Often while I was speaking onstage, memories from my years in the abortion industry would pop into my mind, making it difficult to choke out the words. And afterward, without fail, a line would form. So many women. So many sad stories. So many tears. And with all that, so much healing.

These women were broken, and they were looking to me to help them heal. Early on, there were moments I thought, *I'm not up to this task. I can't do this. I don't have the ability to provide what they need.* But I soon realized that meeting me was probably the first time these women had had the opportunity to look into the face of a person who had worked inside an abortion facility. They were often still dealing with anger and hurt and feelings of betrayal and victimization by the people who had helped arrange and perform their abortions. They were trying to find a moment of forgiveness with me. Having had an abortion myself helped me understand those feelings, so I felt a responsibility to other women who've had abortions to act—to speak to them. To hear their stories. To listen to them. To validate their feelings. And to try to provide some sort of apology for the people in the industry who did betray, violate, manipulate, and exploit them, because they were never going to hear that apology anywhere else. I realized how much they needed that. And I realized how much *I* needed that.

Over time, as I saw the relief and healing on so many faces, God helped me understand that I'd been right. *I* wasn't up to the task. *I* couldn't do this. *I* didn't have the ability to provide what they needed. But *he* was! *He* could! *He* did! My job was to show up, tell my story, be vulnerable, and make myself available. God's mercy—his fierce and tenacious compassion—did the rest. It penetrated their pain and agony and guilt and shame. It washed away their bitterness. It opened their hearts to truth. With that understanding, my faith grew by leaps and bounds. My sense of wonder and awe at how he was at work in the room filled me with joy and anticipation. And my own wounds continued to heal.

Between speaking engagements, I began to write my story, which I also found to be incredibly healing. Revisiting my past helped me process my experiences and begin to see the big picture of how God had been at work in my life all along, though I'd been oblivious to his purposes until now. I'd always been focused on *my* purposes, *my* goals, *my* ambitions. Now, I found myself wondering what *God's* purposes and plans held for me next.

THREE MONTHS FLEW BY. Then one Sunday morning in January 2010, Doug and I were sitting in church with our three-year-old, Grace, listening to some announcements from the pulpit, when out of the blue something deep stirred in me—dare I call it a voice?—and I suddenly felt absolutely compelled to have a second child. The idea swept over me and left me without a doubt that it was time.

Doug had been wanting to expand our family for some time, but I'd been the holdout. Prior to my dramatic turnaround, I'd been totally absorbed in my career. Truthfully, mothering and nurturing had never come easy to me (more on that later). Since my turning point, I'd been in a whirlwind of drama and change, newfound faith, and speaking and traveling. I'd not given a thought to having another child.

Until now. This morning. In the middle of church. Like a bolt of lightning.

I leaned toward Doug. He noticed and leaned toward me to see what I wanted. I whispered, "I want to get my IUD out."

Doug startled and looked at me baffled, confusion all over his face. "Like, now?" he said.

"Well, no. Tomorrow or something."

"Okay. Can we talk about this after church?"

As we pulled out of the church parking lot, I said, "I really want another baby."

Doug grinned ear to ear while shaking his head in disbelief. "So, what are you going to do?"

"Well, I'm going to get this IUD taken out."

"Well, okay by me!"

The next morning, I called my OB-GYN practice and said to the receptionist, "I need an appointment to get my IUD out."

She offered the first available appointment in three weeks.

"Nope. I need to get it out today," I said. "In fact, can I talk to the nurse?"

The nurse came on the phone, and I said, "I need to get my IUD out today."

She said, "Is there a problem?"

"Nope," I said, "but it needs to come out today."

"I don't think we have any appointments today. But we could probably get you in for an appointment in a few weeks."

"Listen," I said, "this IUD is coming out today. Either I'm going to pull it out or you're going to pull it out. But either way, it's coming out today."

There was a pause, then she said, "Can you come in at one?"

When I arrived for my appointment, the doctor asked, "Why do you want it out?"

I said, "I just don't want to have it anymore. I think I want to have more kids."

She said, "What are you going to do for birth control until you've decided for sure?"

I said, "I don't know. I think we'll use natural family planning (NFP) or something." The truth is, I knew nothing about NFP. I had heard two of my new, dear prolife Catholic friends, Heather and Karen, talk about it.

"I don't have anything to give you on that, but I'm sure you can get some information from the Catholic Church," she said. When the appointment was ending, she said, "If you want to get pregnant, now's the perfect time."

Given those words, Doug and I expected to conceive quickly. But that didn't happen. Therefore, after several months, we found a fine new prolife doctor who walked us through how to use NFP to try to conceive. I never did gain an understanding as to why God had filled me with such a sense of urgency that Sunday. All I knew for certain was that I'd experienced a tremendous sudden shift in my desires, and I felt God's call on me to mother another child.

"ABBY!"

The shouting voice was female, pleading, desperate even, and it stopped me in my tracks. I'd just told my story to a crowd of about ten thousand at the Los Angeles Convention Center, and a security guard was escorting me through back corridors to the green room. This May 2010 prolife event, Unidos por la Vida (United for Life), marked eight months since I'd left Planned Parenthood and was being hosted by actor and screenwriter Eduardo Verástegui. I was the only presenter who had delivered their speech in English, so I'd needed a Spanish translator for the predominantly Hispanic audience. I'd worried a bit how that might affect my connection to the women, but I'd been deeply touched by their rapt attention and thunderous applause.

At the sound of the shouting voice, the guard and I exchanged surprised glances. "I suggest we keep moving," the guard said to me, noticing my hesitation.

"ABBY!"

My heart flooded with empathy at the distress I could hear in the voice. This time I saw where it had come from. Down a long hallway to my right was a metal gate that blocked access to these backstage corridors. There, a few people stood, apparently trying to catch a glimpse behind the scenes. One woman—the one calling my name—had her arms stretched through the gate, waving for me to come to her.

"I'm going to her," I told the guard. "You can stay here. I'll be fine." Nevertheless, he followed me.

I could hear the woman softly crying as I approached. I assumed, from months of experience interacting with audiences after speaking, that she'd had an abortion and she strongly identified with my story and was simply seeking some comforting connection. The part of me that felt called to minister to such women sprang to life. When I reached the gate, she fell into my arms, the bars sandwiched between us. I rubbed her back in comforting strokes.

"What's going on?" I said gently.

"I work for Planned Parenthood," she said, crying.

"You work for them right now?"

"Yes."

"Okay. So, what do you want to do?"

She drew her face out of my shoulder, looked me in the eyes, and said, "I don't want to go back. I *won't* go back."

It's hard to describe what I felt at hearing those words. An instant bond. A sense of camaraderie. A rush of memories of the moment I made that same decision for myself. And an understanding of what she would be up against—guilt, remorse, pressure, alienation. But I felt something else as well—an instant sense of responsibility to her. *What do I do?* I thought. *How do I help her?*

"What's your name?"

"Annette. I don't know where to go. I don't know who to ask for help," she said. "My boyfriend brought me here. He wanted me to hear your story."

She went on to explain that they had planned on getting married, but he had told her, "I won't marry you if you're working at Planned Parenthood."

I smiled. This guy sounded like a keeper. He was really pulling out all the stops. It made me think of how Doug had always challenged my thinking when it came to my work in the abortion industry. He, too, had always been on the side of life.

As if on cue, I saw Eduardo Verástegui some distance down the hallway, so I called to him and he came straight over. After introducing Annette and explaining the situation, I said the only thing that made sense. "The first thing we're going to do is pray together." And so we did. As soon as we finished, my eyes met Annette's and I heard myself saying, "I don't know what to do, but I'm going to help you. So let me make some phone calls."

"DOUG, I'VE TRIED EVERYTHING. I've searched and searched online and just like when I left Planned Parenthood,

I can't find any organization that's dedicated to helping abortion workers or that might be a good resource to help Annette. And I've scoured my small contact list looking for someone in the LA area who I might put her in touch with, but I'm coming up with nothing. I wonder if David Bereit might have some ideas."

David had once been the CEO of Coalition for Life—the organization that had prayed outside my facility for so many years. He'd been a supportive friend, and I knew he was well networked nationwide with the prolife movement. I wasn't.

"Give him a call, Abby," my husband said. "She'll need a job fast and some local people in LA for emotional support."

I was so appreciative that when I'd come home from LA and told Doug about Annette, he was 100 percent with me in the effort to help her. Before saying goodbye to Annette at the convention center, I'd told her that Doug and I could offer some financial support if needed—but I'd said so without checking with him. The good news, Annette had assured me, was that she had some money saved and her boyfriend would help her out. Her biggest concern was finding a new job and the emotional support to recover from her years in the abortion industry. I could certainly understand her situation and wanted to walk with her through it, but I wasn't sure what that might look like across so many miles.

When I called David, he flew into action, made some calls, and soon had Annette connected with the compassionate director of a pregnancy center in the LA area. It felt deeply satisfying to see God's hand at work in her life just as he was in mine and to feel that God had used me in some small way in Annette's journey out of the abortion industry. Annette and I stayed in touch. Within a few months, she was offered a job at the pregnancy center, and she and her boyfriend got engaged. Of all the people God had brought across my path so far, I shared something unique with Annette, for she alone knew what it felt like to escape that culture of death and discover a whole new purpose on the side of life. I wondered, *How many others like us are out there?*

MEANWHILE, Doug and I were puzzled. I'd been so certain that God had called us to expand our family, but after months of trying to conceive, I hadn't. I decided to see a new doctor—one who had been recommended by a few of my new prolife friends. He did some blood work, and we discovered that my hormone levels were askew. The doctor then explained that he didn't want me conceiving for several months, as he didn't want me risking a miscarriage due to my abnormal hormone levels.

What followed was months of charting, testing, and hormone therapy. It felt counterintuitive to purposefully avoid pregnancy at the very time we so badly wanted to conceive, but we understood the reasons.

Spiritually, this was a confusing episode to endure. I thought God had called me to have a second child, and we found ourselves longing to see that fulfilled. Why wasn't it happening? However, this was taking place during a time when I'd never felt so spiritually alive. I loved speaking and ministering to women and was constantly amazed at watching his mercy at work in the lives of so many. So, while I look back now and recall my questioning and longing, I also see that I was falling more and more in love with God. I sensed his compassion *for* me just as I sensed his compassion at work *through* me, which left me in awe.

DOUG AND I RANG in the new year of 2011 with a genuine sense of anticipation that God had good things in store. Medically, it looked hopeful that the hormone therapy was helping. Ministry-wise, speaking engagements were continuing to come in. And my book, *Unplanned*, was set to release in January. Would anyone read it? Would babies' lives be saved? Would women considering abortions decide to give birth? Would women who'd had abortions find healing? I prayed and hoped so.

As correspondence, social media, emails, and reviews came pouring in after the book's release, my joy knew no limits. Expectant women who previously might have chosen abortion did give birth! Babies' lives were saved! Post-abortive women did find healing! But something else was happening as well—something so precious to me that I'd dared not even hope for it. Abortion workers who, like me, had found their work in the abortion industry to be disillusioning, dark, and destructive were being moved to leave their jobs. And they were reaching out to me for advice and help.

"I'm leaving too!"

"I read your book and I left. Now I'm worried about what comes next."

"I'm a single mom. I'm afraid that if I leave right away, I won't have enough food. But how can I stay for even one more day?"

For expectant moms and those healing from abortions, I knew ministries I could refer them to. Places they could get help. But these abortion workers were facing the moral dilemma of doling out death for one more day or leaving immediately—and I had no resources for them. Nowhere to send them. And they needed help fast.

"Doug," I said, "what do we do? I have nothing in place for this."

So, Doug and I would send them a $250 Visa gift card, or we'd write them a check. We'd google jobs for them in their area, and I'd talk to them on the phone. We didn't know what we were doing. But we knew no help was out there for them. I started praying for God to put it on the heart of someone to start a ministry for abortion clinic workers who wanted out. I hoped it would be soon.

A prayer God listened to with a smile on his face.

AS I LOOK BACK on my younger self standing outside my old abortion clinic at ten at night pleading for God's mercy— his undeserved favor and compassion—for the blood on my hands, I want to tell her to listen carefully so she will recognize God's voice calling her into a ministry of mercy. I see so clearly now that his voice was in the falling water in the shower. His voice was in the rejoicing of the two prolifers at the fence. His voice was in the invitations to speak and in the worship service urging her to mother a new child. I want her to know that when she heard Annette desperately shouting her name and the doctor's voice of counsel and encouragement and the voices of her book's readers and the abortion workers who wanted out—she was hearing God's voice calling her into a ministry of mercy.

I urge you, reader, to listen as well. Listen so that you will recognize the call to the mercy that God is speaking through the voices in your own life.

"I will have mercy on whom I have mercy,
    and I will have compassion on whom I have compassion."

It does not, therefore, depend on human desire or effort, but on God's mercy. For Scripture says to Pharaoh: "I raised you up for this very purpose, that I might display my power in you and that my name might be proclaimed in all the earth."

Romans 9:15–17

3

HEALING IN PUBLIC

In January 2011, fifteen months after I left Planned Parenthood, *Unplanned* was published. I found that publicly sharing those intimate memories with readers and receiving their comments about how God was using my story to build their faith brought more healing than I ever imagined possible.

At about that same time, however, came what I remember as my first major public blunder as a prolife advocate. It would prove the point that God's mercy alone (which was abundant), not my own expertise (which was sorely lacking), qualified me for my new role. It would also open my heart to receiving and, in response, giving more of God's mercy.

It happened at the Texas State Capitol. One of my great joys in my first months on the prolife side of the fence was getting involved in promoting prolife legislation for Texas. I was attending what was called a prolife primer—an educational session for prolifers to come to the capitol to hear about bills under consideration and various other legislation of interest. If the primer was being held when the representatives and senators were in session, it was sometimes possible for a bill's author to come speak about it. These events were an opportunity for people to ask questions.

Senator Dan Patrick was the author of an ultrasound bill in the Texas Senate—House Bill 15—requiring that twenty-four hours before an abortion, the abortionist must perform an ultrasound and show the image to the mother. I had confidence this bill would have sweeping effects because I knew from experience that once a woman has seen an ultrasound image of her child, she is far less likely to pursue abortion. Also, the majority of doctors who perform abortions in Texas come into the clinic only one day a week, and some, every other week. Requiring the physicians to be present for two days would mean no profit on the first day. Therefore, it was highly likely that the many clinics using circuit-riding abortionists would stop doing abortions or close, strictly for financial reasons.

Senator Patrick spoke at the primer and drove home his points well. Everybody was excited that the bill would soon be passed—a very big deal. The audience sat at round tables listening and asking questions. This was the first time I'd ever helped with prolife legislation, and I was feeling great. In fact, I'd been asked to speak (after the senator) about my part in the bill and why it was so important.

There was a woman at a front table. I knew her a little bit. We had befriended one another on Facebook and interacted online a few times. She had always been very kind to me. I had assumed she wanted to be friends and had been glad when she told me she was going to be at the primer, so I was happy to see her in the audience.

When Senator Patrick was speaking, she asked him a question about the rape and incest exception in the ultrasound bill (this exception means that the bill would not apply in cases of rape and incest). He gave a traditional prolife response: "We're doing everything we can to save as many as we can, and we will go back for that one percent." The rape and incest exception was not something I'd given a lot of thought to, but I'd heard the explanation "we'll go back" frequently and believed it to be true that these legislators intended, after the bill was in effect, to get it modified to eliminate the exception. The woman didn't challenge him, but it was obvious from her response that she and the little group she was with didn't like his answer. This surprised me.

Then it was my turn to speak. I was excited and spoke passionately about the necessity and effectiveness of the bill. Lives would be saved! I could feel the crowd's excitement and knew they were with me. But I also felt like I needed to support Senator Patrick's response. I even felt a bit defensive on his behalf and thought, *I'm going to help him out.* So, I said, "I know the rape and incest exception came up. I echo what Senator Patrick said—that we are trying to save as many as we can. It's really nothing to be upset about. It's just one percent."

I saw many nods of agreement, which didn't surprise me, because after all, I thought this was what the prolife movement believed. I was just repeating what I had heard. At the end of the event, the same woman came up and gave me a big hug. She was so nice and even shared a bit of her story with me. We agreed we would follow up with each other.

But the next day I received an email from someone I didn't know. It said, "I just wanted to let you know that this is circulating." A video was attached of me speaking at the primer, including my "it's just one percent" statement. That was a surprise, as I hadn't even realized anyone was recording me. And there followed a video of the same woman making scathing remarks about me, declaring that I was still pro-choice and still supported abortion, as evidenced by my statement to not be upset by "just one percent" of abortion's victims. She claimed I was faking everybody out, I hadn't really had a conversion, and so on.

I immediately reached out to her via email and said, "I saw the video. I don't understand. We spoke afterward. You didn't bring any of this up." I wasn't at all prepared for her response.

"You're still pro-choice. You believe I'm better off dead."

Aghast, I said, "No! That's not what I want."

To my horror, the video was being shared like crazy online and was quickly generating tons of condemnation aimed at me. Social media over the previous months had already revealed some suspicion and skepticism about me on the part of a number of vocal prolifers. Was I truly prolife? Did I believe abortion is sometimes okay? Was I really just some disgruntled Planned Parenthood employee looking to cash in on a moment in the spotlight? Was I actually a pro-choice plant looking to infiltrate the prolife ranks and undermine the cause of life? Such speculation coupled with the desire of pro-choicers to discredit me had led to not only some honest questions but also some ugly accusations that were painful to read.

Unplanned had recently come out, so my name was being recognized, and I'd been relieved that some of the skepticism had died down. But now, in a heartbeat, I was getting loads of angry mail from prolifers. Shocked and alarmed, I knew this was bad. I was beside myself, with no clue about what to do. I didn't know how to recover because I honestly didn't have the words. Nobody had taught me, "When this comes up, here is the best way to answer."

Besides, I still didn't think that what I said was wrong. Hadn't Senator Patrick been right? You get the bill signed however you can so you can begin to save who you can. Then you go back to protect those conceived in rape and incest. I'd given no thought as to the ramifications of that statement.

The next day, in the midst of the social media storm blowing up in my face, I received a message from a woman named Rebecca Kiessling. Rebecca led a group called Save the One. I thought, *Great. Another one who hates me.* But to my surprise, her message was very kind.

"Hey, I'm so sorry that you're being crucified like this. I'd love to talk with you," she wrote. "I'm sorry this is happening right now."

Talk about being relieved and grateful! So, I talked to Rebecca on the phone, and she shared her story with me, including the fact that she was conceived in rape. It was eye-opening for me to hear that that 1 percent *was* a big deal. She shared a lot of facts. Like that 87 percent of prolife bills do not have this exception, so exceptions don't have to be the standard. I learned that it is always prolife legislators who put in the rape exception, never the pro-choice legislators, as they don't want the bill at all. I'd never really thought about that before. Rebecca helped me understand that what I had said was not only hurtful to people who had been conceived in rape, but it also set a poor precedent for the prolife movement by basically saying, "Yes, we believe all unborn lives are valuable, except for these."

"Abby," she said, "never once has anyone gone back to protect us." And that was shameful to me. Once a bill has been set, no one has ever gone back and closed that exception. Rebecca, in her kind, merciful way, opened my eyes to a new perspective, and we developed a friendship from that moment on. I will always be so thankful to her for not attacking me along with the mob but for educating me instead—because that is what I needed.

After my conversation with Rebecca, I realized how wrong I had been in saying what I had, so I knew I had to come out with something to apologize for it. Of course, I didn't want people saying, "Oh, she's just doing that because we're calling her out." I really wanted people to see that I was wrong. And I wanted to sincerely apologize, not just do damage control. I wrote something, and Rebecca looked it over. Then I put it out there on my own social media.

Unfortunately, it seemed I just fanned the flames. Some people wrote back and said they agreed with what I said. But there was a certain percentage who, no matter what I said, let me know I was now a villain in their eyes. That was it. There was nothing I could do to change that. Many wrote that they felt it was an insincere apology. I was so sad and discouraged. I really meant my apology and had hoped it would help to bring peace.

It was a terrible time. I needed mercy! And I needed it from my own people.

Then Rebecca went the extra mile for me. In the following weeks when people would post something negative about the incident on social media, she would post my apology and say something like, "Abby and I have become friends. She realizes that she made a mistake. She is now against exceptions in these bills. We just have to educate people that maybe don't understand." She was good about saying, "She's only been in this for two years. Two years ago, she was aborting babies, so give her a break. She's learning." It was helpful to have her voice advocating for me. In God's mercy, having Rebecca go to bat for me was huge.

God then showered even more mercy on me through another prolifer. The week after Rebecca reached out, I heard from a leader who has been in the prolife movement for many years and is well respected. She publicly commended me for making the apology.

Finally, I concluded that I'd just have to show my detractors my newly held beliefs through my actions—my support of particular bills and my lack of support for others—that I'm going to stand against the exception.

On the bright side, all this drama was a good learning experience and taught me to keep my mouth shut when I don't know what to say or haven't done my homework. I'm not always going to have the answers, and that's okay. But it was painful to learn this lesson through public humiliation.

I also realized through this experience that even though I'd been well trained by Planned Parenthood to handle the media (something I'll always be grateful for), handling myself as a prolife communicator would require a different way of talking to the media and the public. I had to become more compassionate. I had to become more sensitive. In doing media for Planned Parenthood, I'd been taught that it was all about the issues. Know your talking points. Take every opportunity to drive your points home.

However, when it comes to the issue of abortion, it's not "all" about the issues. It's about people. It's about hearts. It's about lives and deeply personal experiences. That's a huge difference. I'm so grateful to Rebecca for showing me mercy and modeling how that is done through compassion, kindness, and education.

I'd love to report that I learned my new lessons well and never again blundered my way through the public role I'd been given. Wouldn't that be nice! But anyone who has followed my ministry over these years has seen me mess up—lots of times! I've lost my temper. I've overreacted. I've criticized rather than used constructive communication. I've gone public with hurts and feelings that I should have dealt with privately. The list goes on.

Some people have had mercy on me when I messed up. Other people, not so much. But, hey, we are all works in progress, are we not? And I am chief among those whose progress, at times, seems slow in coming. Maybe that's one reason for my passion for mercy—I need it so much!

Speaking of which, here's another confession. Coming into the prolife movement, I had many ideas about the best ways to reach people and the best things to do and not to do. During my eight years at Planned Parenthood, I'd observed and evaluated the myriad of tactics used by prolife organizations. I saw which ones were more or less effective. So, I came in with the attitude that they're going to really appreciate everything I have to say because I've got a fresh perspective from working inside the clinic—one they don't have. Yes, I know now that this was not only naïve but also arrogant. It's embarrassing even writing this, but I think I was expecting a big, "Well, thank you so much, Abby!"

So, imagine my surprise when I discovered in my first and second year on the side of life that many prolifers really didn't want to hear from me. Or they took the posture, "Girl, you don't know what you're talking about. You're new to this. Let us handle it. We've been doing it for over thirty years. We know what we're doing."

I thought that was like saying, "I've been in the ninth grade fifteen times, so I'm the best at it," while I was thinking, *No, you have to move forward. You have to progress.* I saw many things being done the same as they had been thirty years ago, and I thought, *That's not moving forward. That's not keeping up with the women we're trying to reach.* I'd see prolife people or organizations doing something that didn't make sense to me, and I would call them out on social media. Instead of understanding that people are going to do things differently and the prolife movement is as varied and complex as the pro-abortion culture, I'd be critical. I believed I was being helpful, simply trying to "enlighten" those who knew no better. Like I said, naïve and arrogant, right?

Fortunately, God wasn't content to leave me in that state. In order for me to learn that publicly judging and criticizing my fellow prolifers was not only counterproductive but also hurtful, he wisely allowed the tables to be turned on me.

"I don't understand how any woman can abort her child," a young woman spat out angrily at me one day. "It's murder, no matter what the circumstances. Only a selfish, heartless woman would do such a thing."

You'd think I would have been used to such statements, having heard every condemnation under the sun uttered over the years outside my abortion clinic. But this time it was different. This time I wasn't on the opposite side of the fence from the hateful rhetoric. This woman and I were on the same side. Allies. Or so I had assumed.

I physically recoiled at her words on two levels. First, as a prolife advocate, I believe in offering hope, healing, and help to abortion-minded women, not condemnation. I wanted to distance myself from this woman and her rhetoric. I didn't want anyone—prolife or pro-choice—to hear her harsh words. I was embarrassed to be associated with her and her mindset. Secondly, on a far more personal level, I felt I'd been kicked in the stomach. I'd had two abortions myself, and now that I'd become prolife, I was still working through healing from them.

I see now that I was healing on my own but in front of hundreds of thousands of people. And some of my pain came out as arrogance. I wanted people to believe I was okay. I needed them to believe that. I felt like I had to right the wrongs for the twenty-two thousand aborted babies I had helped kill. I had to save as many babies as possible. Maybe if I perfected the prolife movement, that would be enough?

As I was writing the manuscript for *Unplanned*, I realized that I still needed healing from my past abortions, so I went through just about every Bible study on the topic I could lay my hands on, and I healed a little bit more with each one. I eventually came to the place I hope you can come to concerning God's mercy over your past sins. I owned the fact that those abortions were wrong, and I regretted and grieved both of those decisions. In doing so, I moved through the three choices regarding mercy that I briefly mentioned in chapter 1—to truly recognize mercy, to fully receive mercy, and to generously give mercy. I *recognized* God's mercy at work on the cross, as it paid for the wrong of those abortions. I prayed to fully *receive* that mercy so I could move on from those memories, those two grievous choices. Finally, I felt motivated to reflect God's mercy by *giving* that mercy to others. This kind of healing is what I now wanted for every woman who had ever had an abortion.

However, if I did not want to be judged by others for my abortions, how could I continue to judge other prolifers for their choices? I had to learn to show them mercy. I could begin by keeping my head down and continuing to do what God had called me to do. I reminded myself that my job was not to tell everybody else how to do theirs. I am responsible for doing my job. If others are excelling or getting great results, then perhaps I should try their methods too. If other people are watching me and they see good results, they may choose to follow in my footsteps. I've found it's more powerful to influence by example than by calling them out and telling them they're not doing something right. Because if they react defensively, they're less likely to reevaluate what they are doing. I came to realize that we need more allies than enemies in this movement. I had to accept that our allies are not always going to make the same choices we do, or have the same beliefs or experiences, or utilize the same tactics—and that's okay. They're still our allies in this fight.

In addition to showing mercy by example, I found it's important to be vulnerable and authentic. We all struggle with something. I can identify with your struggle, and you can identify with mine. Over sixty million abortions have taken place in this country. That accounts for a lot of women who need God's mercy for their choices. And that doesn't even begin to take into consideration the millions who need God's mercy for other reasons. There's so much hurt in our world. We are not alone in our own pain. We are walking in the midst of a huge number of wounded people. We don't have to pretend to be perfect or try to hide our wounds. If we want to be part of the work of God's mercy in the world, we don't want to hide who we really are. We want to be truly authentic. We all long to hear that we're not alone, and authenticity demonstrates that.

Participating in the prolife movement meant I was part of something bigger than myself. Really loving people and intentionally trying to love them to the best of my ability, showing mercy, and being authentic are practical ways I could begin to love people well.

I found that I could help prolifers, like this woman who had spoken to me so harshly, better understand abortion-inclined women, abortion workers, and women who'd had abortions. I was surprised how often I heard a prolifer say, "I don't understand how anybody could have an abortion." Now I could answer their questions by helping them consider a woman who has only known abortion as a viable choice to a pregnancy or who is feeling pressured by her boyfriend or who is being told she's getting kicked out of her house if she doesn't have an abortion or who has no money to raise a child or who already has four other children and is a single mom and doesn't know how she's going to make it.

The same principles apply to how we speak of and respond to abortion workers. I would hear people say, "I don't want to help anybody who worked in an abortion clinic." I could now help them consider the plight of someone who had barely been making ends meet until they landed a fantastic job that provided them with benefits, including health insurance, and gave them time off for their kids (many workers, in my observation, are single moms), all while paying a wage they would never find anywhere else.

One thing I found myself trying to do with my story was help people understand that it could have been them. It could have been anybody who, by making a series of difficult choices, found themselves walking through the doors of that clinic as a patient or worker (or both, like me). And so, part of what I began doing, hopefully with the same heart and tactics as Rebecca Kiessling, was kindly educating people on the *why*. *Why* would someone work in an abortion clinic? *Why* would a woman choose abortion? If we really want to reach these workers and women, we must begin to listen to their stories in order to understand their choices. If we catch ourselves falling into thinking, *I don't know how she could do* . . . or *I don't know how anybody could ever* . . . then we may want to train ourselves instead to think, *It's not for me to understand someone else's sin. It's for me to understand forgiveness. And it's for me to understand and offer mercy and compassion.*

OVER THE PAST ten years, as I've been healing in public, many people who have heard my conversion story have said to me, "Abby, your story is just like Saul becoming Paul!" Well, I wouldn't place myself in such illustrious company, but it's certainly true that everyone loves a good conversion story. Saving the one. Going after the lost. The thief on the cross. Welcoming home the prodigal. And so on. My conversion is, likewise, a dramatic turnaround story that lifts the heart.

But I see another parallel in the Saul to Paul story that I'd like you to consider because it might apply to you. You see, many people never have that big, dramatic moment of being struck down off their horse. And so they wrongly assume they can't have a big, dramatic ministry. I think what's far more important than that falling-off-the-horse moment is what happened next—a follower of Jesus showed up to help Paul move from the darkness into the light. And that person was Ananias.

I love the story as it's told in Acts 9. As it opens, I do see myself in Saul, for it says, "Saul was still breathing out murderous threats against the Lord's disciples" (v. 1). Yes, that was me at my clinic, breathing out murderous threats against the prolifers praying outside and carrying out murderous plans against babies inside the clinic. So, in verse 2, Saul was delivering letters to the synagogues of Damascus that gave him the authority to imprison any there "who belonged to the Way [Christian believers], whether men or women, [that] he might take them as prisoners to Jerusalem."

Suddenly a bright light from heaven appeared, knocking him off his horse, and a voice said, "Saul, Saul, why do you persecute me?" (v. 4). Saul asked who was speaking to him, and he heard a voice. "'I am Jesus, whom you are persecuting,' he replied. 'Now get up and go into the city, and you will be told what you must do'" (vv. 5–6).

When Saul got up from the ground and opened his eyes, he found that he was blind. Paul's companions led him to Damascus, and for three days, Paul, still blind, waited and prayed.

Meanwhile, across town, the Lord spoke in a vision to a disciple of his named Ananias. The Lord told him, "Go to the house of Judas on Straight Street and ask for a man from Tarsus named Saul, for he is praying. In a vision he has seen a man named Ananias come and place his hands on him to restore his sight" (vv. 11–12).

Can you relate to the first thing Ananias did? Assuming God must be mistaken, he *informed* God of the facts! Ananias answered, "Lord . . . I have heard many reports about this man and all the harm he has done to your holy people in Jerusalem. And he has come here with authority from the chief priests to arrest all who call on your name" (vv. 13–14).

The Lord said, "Go! This man is my chosen instrument to proclaim my name to the Gentiles and their kings and to the people of Israel" (v. 15).

Ananias then made a very wise decision—he did what God told him to do. "Then Ananias went to the house and entered it. Placing his hands on Saul, he said, 'Brother Saul, the Lord—Jesus, who appeared to you on the road as you were coming here—has sent me so that you may see again and be filled with the Holy Spirit'" (v. 17).

And God used Ananias's obedience in a huge way. "Immediately, something like scales fell from Saul's eyes, and he could see again. He got up and was baptized, and after taking some food, he regained his strength" (vv. 18–19). Then, of course, Saul, renamed Paul by the Lord shortly thereafter, went on to take the gospel to the gentiles and became the most prolific writer of the New Testament.

You don't have to be a Paul to make a difference in our culture or to carry God's mercy into this world and into people's hearts. You don't have to have some major moment when you are struck down off your horse. The person who prayed for Paul so that the scales fell from his eyes was just as important.

And that person was Ananias.

Everyone doesn't have a fall-off-your-horse conversion experience. But everybody does, like me, blunder and fall and need an Ananias. If you are ever tempted to think, *I don't have a big conversion story. What can I do?* I say, "You be Ananias. Because Paul would have been nothing if he hadn't had Ananias!"

Rebecca Kiessling was my Ananias. She came to me. She reached out to me with mercy. She compassionately educated me and then spoke up for me to others.

Be someone's Ananias!

We're going to continue to explore how mercy happens and how it can be woven into your life so it flows to others. No matter your past or what you've been involved with, your failures, or whatever you fear may stand in your way, I want you to discover and trust that God's mercy is always there, always waiting, and always available. You, like Ananias, can always be a channel through which God's mercy flows into the lives of others.

> We have different gifts, according to the grace given to each of us. If your gift is prophesying, then prophesy in accordance with your faith; if it is serving, then serve; if it is teaching, then teach; if it is to encourage, then give encouragement; if it is giving, then give generously; if it is to lead, do it diligently; if it is to show mercy, do it cheerfully.
>
> Romans 12:6–8

4

DANGEROUS
PRAYERS

'd love to tell you that discovering and falling in love with God's mercy is like a steady, progressive journey from the shallows of new faith to the depths of maturity, each step forward just a tad deeper than the one before, like wading into a placid lake until you are swimming in deep waters. That does sound nice. And who knows, for some people that may be the case. But not for me.

My journey of spiritual growth and discovery—of experiencing God's mercy so deeply that I longed to reflect it—was far more like jumping from an ocean liner into the depths of the sea. I did a lot of flailing around, gasping for air, riding huge waves, and tumbling in all directions, not sure which direction was up or forward. If that sounds terrifying, in a way it was, because I was a woman who, up until that ultrasound, had been so sure of myself, my direction, and my ability to navigate my own life to reach my desired future. By contrast, I'd plunged into this ocean that offered no self-determining control—a dangerous place for someone who wanted to believe she could control her own destiny.

On the one hand, the uncertainty of where I was headed long-term was terrifying and unnerving. On the other, it was exhilarating, adventurous, and amazingly freeing. The 2009 unmasking of Planned Parenthood's true values and the subsequent witnessing of the ultrasound had convinced me that the ocean liner I'd chosen was headed in the wrong direction, where certain disaster awaited. It was far safer to cast myself into the sea and there discover where God would take me. After all, God rules over the sea. As the psalmist in Psalm 89:9 writes,

> You rule over the surging sea;
> when its waves mount up, you still them.

Once I took the plunge, it was up to God where I would go next. Psalm 135:6 puts it all in perspective:

> The Lord does whatever pleases him,
> in the heavens and on the earth,
> in the seas and all their depths.

For the first time in my life, I really wanted to do whatever would please God.

In my first year and a half as a prolifer, as I thought about pleasing God, I reasoned, *I don't know what God's calling me to do in the long run. I don't know what the bigger plan for me—if there is a bigger plan—might be. Maybe I'm going to work at a grocery store for the next twenty years. I have no idea. For now, I'm just telling my story to whoever will listen.*

It seemed at every turn I found a camera or a microphone, and I simply responded by telling the story of what God had done in my life. That sense of purpose carried me into 2011.

But as 2011 took shape, Doug and I had to face some pretty big decisions, and I desperately wanted to make the "right" ones. What would I do about a new career? Would I keep speaking? How long would the invitations keep coming? And if they did, how were we to manage Grace's care and her beginning preschool when I was away from home (she was now four, turning five in November)? And what of Doug's career as a public schoolteacher? We both felt it was time for a major change there. Also, what was God up to in my continued infertility? Why had God instilled this intense desire in me for a second child if not to conceive? Had I misunderstood him? And meanwhile, as more and more people read my book, not only were babies' lives being saved, but more abortion workers, like Annette, were reaching out to me wanting help. I'd begun praying earnestly in early 2010 for God to raise up someone with a heart to minister to former abortion workers—someone I could refer these workers to.

All these matters formed the basis of what was becoming a lively prayer life—something that was still quite new to me. In my past, I'd seen prayer as something one does formally before a meal or during church—or something done more by rote, like the reading of prayers in the liturgy during a worship service. But now that I understood that I was a living, breathing example of answered prayer, and since I'd been traveling and speaking at so many Christian events and seeing prayer in action, my prayer life was starting to reflect what I was witnessing time and time again—prayer was a vibrant conversation with the living God. Philippians 4:6 had a huge impact on me: "Do not be anxious about anything, but in every situation, by prayer and petition, with thanksgiving, present your requests to God." So, I took God at his word and began presenting him with my many requests. The "do not be anxious" part, however, was a bit more challenging. I tended to be anxious *and* pray.

Even so, presenting my requests to God and actually expecting him to answer are two different things. When *Unplanned* came out, I prayed that clinic workers, people who still worked in the industry, would pick up the book and read it—maybe as a critic. I never minded a critical reader. After all, if I were still working in the clinic and some former worker wrote a tell-all book about the industry, I'd read it. I'd want to know what they were saying. My hope was that people would read *Unplanned* and find some truth in it. And that truth would compel them to leave. I didn't really know if it would happen. In fact, I prayed, not really thinking it would happen but hoping that it might.

But God surprised me. Within five months of the book's release, Doug and I had already helped seventeen workers! They had all read the book. And they had all wanted out of the industry. Many of them emailed me and said, "I could have written some of that myself. It is my story too. I know what you're going through. I also want to leave. Can you help me?" Just as I had when I first encountered Annette and felt compelled to help her, I looked around and thought, *Prolife people have been fighting to end abortion for almost forty years. Surely there must be an organization out there somewhere for abortion clinic workers.* I didn't want to reinvent the wheel. I simply wanted to plug them into an existing ministry and then come alongside to help however I could. But when I realized no such ministry existed, I prayed, "God, please put it on someone's heart to minister to abortion workers—to reach out to them with compassion. Just let that person know that's what they're supposed to do." It didn't occur to me that the someone might be me. I didn't know how to start a nonprofit. I didn't know how to get an organization going from the ground up. I didn't know how to run one. And I certainly didn't have any money to do it.

Sometime during 2011, I began to realize that my involvement with the prolife movement would not be temporary. I felt a strong desire and commitment to always be part of it in some way; I was destined to play some role. I didn't know exactly what that was going to look like, but I knew from observation during my traveling and speaking that we—prolifers as a whole—weren't loving people the way they needed to be loved. We were making a lot of judgments about the women walking into clinics and the workers in the abortion industry. I couldn't shake the sense that my calling at its essence was coming alongside people touched in some way by abortion and trying to love them well.

Something has to change here, I thought, *and I want to play a part in bringing that change.* As I encountered anger, judgment, and resentment within the movement, I thought back to my early days in the abortion industry, before 40 Days for Life worked so hard to change the tone on the sidewalk, when ugly chants and signs accused workers and women who'd had abortions of being murderers. Thanks to the peaceful prayer vigils and loving efforts of those who befriended and prayed for me, a healing and loving tone was established—which is the very reason I'd turned to 40 Days for Life when I hit my personal turnaround point. Now I wanted to inspire that same tone in others so that even more people would be loved onto the side of life.

IN THE SUMMER OF 2011, Doug and I moved from College Station to Austin, Texas. The idea was that Grace would be starting school and Doug would find a teaching job there. But frankly, he wasn't feeling excited about going back to teaching even though that was his field—the only kind of grown-up work he'd ever done. One of us suggested (we still don't recall which of us) that Doug stay home with Grace. If he went to work while I was still speaking, we were going to have to find a preschool or another daycare arrangement for her. So, we decided he'd stay home for the coming school year and see how it worked and if he even liked it. He could put his teaching skills to work by homeschooling Grace. The idea quickly took root for both of us.

Looking back now, I can see how God was laying the groundwork for another area of major growth for me, though I didn't see it coming at the time. But that's what happens when we pray. God often (dare I say *usually*) works in ways we never imagine. And in our case, we really needed some major growth, because the truth of the matter was that our marriage had some significant unresolved issues that were eating away at us.

If you would have asked me at the time, I would have identified our biggest problem as my "workaholism." I saw this addiction to work as a holdover from my Planned Parenthood days. Our marriage had really suffered from my work at Planned Parenthood. I think part of the issue was that at the clinic, marriage was not seen as a good thing. When Doug and I got married in 2005, my boss asked, "Are you sure you want to get married? Why are you getting married?" Likewise, having children was also not seen as a good thing. "I can take care of that for you," my boss said when she realized I was pregnant with Grace, indicating her willingness to schedule an abortion for me at our clinic. Marriage and children were viewed as distractions that would take a woman away from her focus on work and her own dreams.

So, I had worked very hard to prove that they were not distractions for me. For years, even on the weekends, I put in very long hours. Even on Sundays after we'd go to church, I would go to the office for the rest of the day. I had assumed that once I had Grace, those hours would decrease, but that didn't happen. In fact, they increased. It was nothing for me to spend sixty to seventy hours a week at the clinic.

But now that I was praying such "dangerous" prayers as asking to conceive another child and for God to enrich our marriage, I began to understand that my overinvestment in work went far deeper than the Planned Parenthood influences. Work, I slowly realized, was an escape for me because I didn't know how to be a mom to Grace. I found mothering to be a struggle. I was often depressed when I was with her—a holdover from my severe postpartum depression, which I wrote about in *Unplanned*. Work was my escape from those feelings of uncertainty, self-doubt, and depression. I'd always known what to do with myself at work. I did not know what to do as a mom with Grace. I realized that I resented her because I feared that parenting her would take away some of my freedom. Doug and I had been fighting about this for some time.

The challenge, however, was that my new "job" of speaking left me wide open to the same temptation to bury myself in the busyness of work. It was not uncommon for me to speak at fifteen events a month. And after the publication of my book, staying on top of all my emails and social media could be a full-time job if I let it. And I had such a tendency to let it.

There was also an unspoken reality that I began to come to grips with. Over time, I had greatly emasculated Doug. I felt an intense drive to be in charge—to be the leader of the house. And to top it off, I'd been absent for years. I'd left him to care for Grace alone. My actions and attitudes had really worn on our marriage. I had not relinquished to Doug any headship of our home, spiritual or otherwise. And I knew better, because I grew up in a home where healthy headship was modeled for me. I knew what that looked like, but I was not allowing it in my home.

As my eyes were opened, I saw that we had years of damage to work through. Fortunately, thanks to prayer, rather than feeling hopeless or discouraged, I began to feel a sense of expectation and hope. If God could change me like he already had, then surely he could change our marriage too. Doug and I agreed that we both wanted to break out of old negative patterns and build a Christ-centered relationship.

ONE OF OUR FIRST PRIORITIES in Austin was to find a new church home, and we wasted no time getting started. Sunday after Sunday we visited all manner of churches. In some we were struck by a welcoming friendliness, in others we felt invisible and unnoticed, and a few times we felt like we'd shown up as uninvited guests to a private club. It's amazing the variety of personalities that churches can have. Fortunately, Doug and I were on the same page as to what we were looking for. The denominational label held little interest for us. We wanted to hear messages from the pulpit based on the Word of God and expressed in such a way that we'd feel personally challenged and inspired to grow in our commitment and ability to live out of faith. We also wanted a worship experience that centered on the majesty, mystery, and holiness of God.

We knew we were on the right track when we found a church that we wanted to return to again and again. Interestingly, it was a Catholic church. Neither of us had grown up Catholic, so much was new to us, but since the prolife movement is heavily populated by Catholics and we'd been moving in those circles since 2009, we felt a familiarity with it. As only God would have it, the topic of marriage was addressed on a number of occasions, and each time, I felt God was speaking directly to Doug and me. I appreciated how marriage was addressed in terms of a solemn sacrament, a lifelong commitment not only to one another but to God as well—and never something to casually step into or out of. That helped me see my relationship with Doug as having time—a lifetime—to grow stronger with God's help.

This inspired me to read some books on marriage. I was struck by the view echoed from the pulpit that when we commit to a spouse, there is almost a trinitarian union with us, our spouse, and God. That was new to me as well. It was as if God was shining a light directly on my struggle to let go of the reins in our home. I saw that God had put Doug in the role of leader in our home and that I had to get out of the way so Doug could take that role. This was a lesson in humility for me as I realized that I may not have all the answers. I have a take-charge personality—always have. But I had to get serious about allowing him to exercise his leadership. This would take a lot of communication, which was also new because I had never communicated with Doug very well. I tended to tell far more than dialogue and listen. That had to change for him to assume the leadership role he already had the desire to exercise. So, our marriage needed a lot of healing. Healing that would take place only if we worked together with Christ as the head of our home. This godly perspective needed to become a whole new way of life for us both.

One Sunday, the pastor spoke about the importance of praying for each other in marriage, and it hit me like a bolt of lightning that I'd never really prayed for Doug before! So, I began to pray for his relationship with God, his role as leader, and his purity of heart. Those prayers drew me spiritually and emotionally closer to Doug.

Now I see something that I didn't see at the time: what was happening between Doug and me was a mirror reflection of what was going on between me and God as well. I needed to stop blustering through life as if I was in charge of everything. God was in charge! And I needed to live accordingly.

Sunday morning teachings were also opening my eyes on the role of parenthood—of nurturing the hearts and souls of those children God might give us. This message pierced me in two ways. First, it brought home the point I'd already begun focusing on in my struggle with working too many hours. It stirred in me a greater desire to spend focused time with Grace—to invest in my vocation of motherhood. Secondly, it reinforced my desire to have another child, and so I redoubled my prayers that God would allow us to conceive.

By fall of 2011, rather than feeling discouraged by my continued infertility, I found myself filled with anticipation and hope yet waiting on God to do what only God could do. In the meantime, a few more abortion workers reached out to me for help. Doug and I prayed for them and about them. I spoke to them at length multiple times on the phone, counseled them on job hunting, and gave them gift cards to ease some of the financial pinch while they hunted for jobs. I found myself feeling a nurturing instinct toward them similar to the one I felt toward Grace and my yet-to-be-conceived child—anticipation and hope. In addition to my commitment to building a healthier marriage, these two issues—wanting to conceive and wanting God to raise up someone to help assist abortion workers in leaving their jobs—filled my prayers.

God's timetable is seldom the same as our own. As countless Christians will attest, there are times when God seems to thrust us into situations we feel unprepared to handle, just as there are times God takes years to grant the thing for which we have an immediate desire. Only God knows the perfect timing of his plans for us.

You, too, may feel like I did in the beginning of 2011—tossed about in the waves of an unknown future, tumbling in all directions and not sure which direction is up or forward. I've certainly felt it since then and expect I'll feel it again in this life. The simple truth is that we are not in charge. Nor should we be. We don't have the wisdom, the perspective, the experience, or the knowledge to call the shots on what goes down in our lifetime. But we do have a great privilege—the privilege of prayer. I've come to believe in daring prayer, dangerous prayer. And with a nod to the title of this book—remembering that *fierce* means marked by unrestrained zeal, intense, furiously active, and highly determined—fierce prayer. May you be fierce in the requests you take before our God! But as you are, keep in mind that his mercy—while it is divine, undeserved favor and compassion—is designed not to give us all we want when we want it but to serve his purposes in his perfect timing.

In the case of my prayers, November 2011 brought a season of spectacular thanksgiving. Doug and I discovered that, after a year and a half of waiting, I was pregnant and would give birth in July. In the midst of our joyful celebration, Doug announced that he loved being a stay-at-home dad while I did my prolife speaking, so we agreed he'd continue when the new baby arrived. We'd found our church home. And for now, at least, my "job" was still to travel and tell the story of the power, the meaning, and the sanctity of human life.

And finally, deep in my spirit, a new certainty took hold. God had *already* answered my prayer that he would raise up someone with the passion and conviction to reach out to abortion workers, invite them out of their abortion work, and help them establish a new life. *I was that someone!*

> Let us then approach God's throne of grace with confidence, so that we may receive mercy and find grace to help us in our time of need.
>
> Hebrews 4:16

5

THE VICTIM AND THE VICTIMIZER

'm thinking of launching a new ministry organization," I said to a friend as we chatted at our local coffee shop. "It's kind of daunting, so I'll be looking for a core group of supporters to provide advice and encouragement. Since you're a leader in the prolife movement, I thought of you."

"Thanks for thinking of me, Abby. That's exciting." She set down her coffee and leaned forward, eagerness transforming her expression. "What would be the focus of your ministry?"

I smiled at her anticipation. "I really feel called to help abortion workers quit their jobs and find new careers outside the abortion industry."

Her eager expression faded, replaced by an involuntary grimace. For the first time since we'd sat down, silence hung between us. I waited. She squirmed.

"Not what you expected?" I finally asked with a nervous laugh, wanting to break the awkward silence.

She pushed her coffee cup to the side, looked at me, and took a deep breath. "Well, not really. I mean, considering the many needs in the prolife movement, why help abortion workers, of all people?" Her voice gathered conviction. "Let them fend for themselves. If they really want out, they'll find a way. After all, they aren't the victims. It's the victimized mothers and babies who need our help. Besides, Abby, people aren't going to come out of that line of work in any significant numbers—not enough to make a difference in this battle."

I winced. I was only one person who'd come out of that line of work. Wasn't I making a difference in this battle of life and death? I hoped so.

My heart fell as I considered her reasoning—not because it surprised me, but because it didn't. In fact, most of the prolife leaders I'd told of my dream for a new kind of ministry had responded in similar ways—even some who were my biggest advocates.

"It will never work, Abby."

"You'll never be able to raise support for that cause."

"These workers are never going to come to us. They'll never trust us enough."

"Why help the victimizers? It's the victims we need to help."

Yet the more I heard such responses, the more I felt God telling me, "That hopelessness is a lie."

Maybe it was the rebel in me, maybe it was the calling I felt, or perhaps it was a little of both, but whatever it was caused me to dig in my heels and say, "I'm doing it." It was as though the more naysayers I encountered, the more I felt God knocking on my heart and saying, "You prayed for someone. You *are* that someone. I have planted this vision in you. So, get it done."

After the discouraging conversation with my friend at the coffee shop, I came home and told Doug, "I feel I really need to make this ministry happen soon. But I have nothing—no model—to refer to. It's not like starting a pregnancy center, where I could ask around for advice. I could call any of a thousand pregnancy centers and say, 'Can you give me your protocols? How do you do it? What do you do first?' But for this, there is no one to call. No resources to give me ideas or guide me."

Doug said, "It sounds like you need reinforcement—a helper by your side. Who might be a good fit?"

It was a good idea. I ended up enlisting Jennie, a young woman I knew who had a heart for abortion workers. She was just out of college and very motivated. I knew I could give Jennie a task, and she would get it done. That's what I needed, because I felt stuck trying to figure out how to start a nonprofit, develop a mission, do fundraising, and build a team. Jennie and I got started by pulling together information on how to set up a 501(c)(3).

I named the ministry And Then There Were None (ATTWN) because that was my dream—that so many workers would leave the industry that abortion facilities would have to cut back on abortions or even close their doors. Everyone who quit would leave a gap that would need to be filled. I knew from experience at my own Planned Parenthood clinic how much time and energy it took to hire and train the workers, using clinic resources that would have otherwise been spent on luring more women in to have abortions.

The plan was for ATTWN to provide services to abortion workers who felt dissatisfied in their jobs, helping them find new fulfilling and positive careers. This would include provision for their practical and financial needs, job counseling, or whatever they needed to help them get back on their feet and go in a new direction. Even more importantly, if we took care in how we ministered to these workers, we might have the opportunity to introduce them to Jesus Christ—the greatest benefit of all! Just the thought of it made my heart pound harder. This idea was bold yet practical, spiritual yet tangible.

Of course, all those great big-picture plans meant I had a lot of specifics to work out, including not only how ATTWN would function but also how we'd finance it. New ideas were coming quickly, thanks to the fairly regular emails and Facebook messages I was getting from workers reaching out for help and counsel after reading my book. For this reason, I felt a sense of urgency to get started. We'd fly by the seat of our pants and figure out details as we went along, but we could at least get started helping abortion workers break away.

Soon a plan began to take shape. Jennie and I would launch the organization on June 12, 2012, using a live webcast to celebrate, get the word out, and raise support. I once again reached out to David Bereit, my friend who'd led webcasts for 40 Days for Life. He graciously agreed to help.

I did have to marvel at the timing. I was due to give birth to my second child in July. I felt that after all my time waiting and praying for a child and for this ministry, it seemed only fitting that both would be "delivered" in the same season. My anticipation for new ministry and new motherhood was running sky-high.

WHEN I AWOKE on launch day, I felt like I was about to burst with excitement. Though David had helped us with all the behind-the-scenes planning, Jennie and I would be live on the webcast. I was excited to share our vision for what And Then There Were None could accomplish in the lives of abortion workers. I was also eager to see how our viewers would respond to that vision and decide to contribute to it.

We'd set what seemed to us to be a reasonable financial goal, modeled after what I knew some other prolife webcasts had earned in live webcasts. (We figured we would earn about 50 percent of what a modest prolife webcast might bring in.) Now we would discover how reasonable our goal was. We'd also set our expectations based on the assumption that over the first year, maybe ten to twelve abortion workers would hear our message, seek our services, and leave the abortion industry for good. We would consider that super successful.

I'd participated in fundraisers as part of my old job at Planned Parenthood, but this event felt dramatically different. Because on this day, instead of asking people to contribute to a billion-dollar organization, I'd be asking them to trust *me* with their investment. It was an audacious request. How did they know I wasn't going to take off with their money for a worldwide cruise? I was asking for a lot of trust.

At the end of the event, we were grateful for every dollar we raised, though it was barely 22 percent of our goal. Clearly, we'd overestimated expected contributions. But the results made sense when we thought about it. When you donate to a pregnancy center, you are sent pictures of precious little babies you have helped save. It makes you feel good to know you have participated in those babies' lives. Our donors would get no such reward. We would have no babies to show them. Instead, they might get anonymous stories of former clinicians who now had a relationship with God but didn't want their faces shown.

As I write this, I am deeply moved at the memory of those donors, many of whom still support us years later. Each one is part of my heart because they believed in us when very few people did. They gave to us before ever seeing results. I had no stories to share with them and nothing to give them, but they saw the vision. They saw what *could* happen, and they gave.

Though we'd overestimated the contributions from donors, we quickly learned that we'd underestimated the response we would receive from abortion workers. Our very first abortion worker called our phone number the next day. The second called only a week later. And by the end of our first year, June 2013? Ten? Fifteen? Twenty abortion workers? Not even close. Fifty-six abortion workers responded to our services and left the abortion industry for good!

We therefore faced an interesting challenge—there was a proven hunger for our services, and we had an extremely limited budget from which to serve people. Clearly, running ATTWN was going to be a faith-growing endeavor requiring creativity and resourcefulness on our part. Somehow, I didn't flinch. I believe that's because my sense of calling was so strong that I didn't doubt God was in charge. I didn't have to ask myself, *Should I be doing this?* "Yes!" was the resounding answer before I even asked the question.

I'M SO GRATEFUL to the Lord for the personal conviction and confidence I had that ATTWN was born from his heart, then planted in mine. Otherwise, I could have been deeply shaken by one aspect of the unexpected response to our launch. It came from a source I would not have expected—

other prolifers. I found that painful and confusing. The issue? An argument that we *shouldn't* be reaching out to help abortion workers.

I'd understood the skepticism and challenges I'd heard from many prolifers when I first shared my vision. After all, ATTWN didn't fit the mold of other prolife ministries. We weren't a pregnancy center helping moms in crisis and saving the lives of babies. We weren't a sidewalk ministry praying outside of abortion centers. We weren't lobbyists fighting pro-abortion legislation and promoting prolife policy. We weren't a home for unwed moms. Our sole focus was on the hearts, minds, and souls of those working in abortion facilities. What I wasn't prepared for was the immediate backlash.

When I would post information about our ministry on my Facebook page, about 75 percent of the comments people posted were along the lines of, "They killed babies. I'm glad it's hard for them to make ends meet. I'm glad it's hard for them to get a job. You shouldn't be making it any easier for them."

I saw this as a very punitive belief that ran contrary to Jesus's message and ministry. Jesus was not punitive in dealing with the tax collectors, the prostitutes, the adulterers, the thieves who hung by his sides as he gave his life for us. He was merciful. Think of the woman caught in adultery, of Matthew and Zacchaeus, of the tax collectors, of the woman at the well. He was invitational. He reached out to them to draw them to himself. His concern was not to "make them pay" but rather that he would pay for their sins with his death on the cross. Wasn't it our calling to follow Jesus's example?

It was frustrating. Because here they were on *my* Facebook page. I wanted to say, "You know what *I* did. You know who *I* am. You're on here *because* of my platform—the fact that

I used to work at an abortion clinic. That's one of the very reasons people want to hear my story. So, if you like the story of what God did in my life, why are you wanting to punish these other workers?"

Another common comment was along the lines of, "Sure, you may get a few workers out, but you're not saving any babies. We're about saving babies." I struggled to find a loving way to say back, "But don't we also care about saving souls? Why are we comparing ministries as if one is better than the other? Surely the body of Christ has room to minister to different people in different ways."

I perceived, rightly or wrongly, that the real motivation behind some of these comments was a spirit of competition over donors. It appeared that some feared ATTWN might siphon away their own base of financial contributors, and this saddened me. I believe that when God calls one of his people to serve in ministry, we need to celebrate his work being done and trust him to motivate people to give generously to fund that work as he sees fit. Jealousy of other ministries only demonstrates our lack of faith in God as the provider.

Frankly, these responses to the birth of ATTWN gave me some spiritual work to do—I had to pray that God would make me merciful to those who espoused these views rather than get angry and want to publicly correct them. My focus needed to be on following God's lead, not worrying over the views of others. I needed to respect the role of the Holy Spirit to convict and redirect as needed. That was his calling, not mine.

However, I did come to acknowledge that part of my calling was to be a wave-maker within the prolife community. As I got to know our support base, I realized we were not appealing to many of the same donors as those of the general

prolife movement because our ministry called for a slightly
different way of thinking. My experience had taught me that
the true "cost" of abortion in our culture went far beyond the
number of babies lost, as horrific as that was. The cancer of
abortion ate away at more than that. It ate away at the hearts
and consciences of women who'd had abortions, abortionists, abortion technicians and administrators, abortion ac-
countants, abortion fundraisers, and abortion contributors.
And it likely poisoned their families as it had poisoned mine.
All these lives—*eternal* lives—were worth fighting for. *All*
these lives were *just* as valuable as life in the womb.

I quickly learned that saying so was not popular among
some prolifers.

I do feel called to say this: Each of us, according to the
leading of the Holy Spirit, needs to be obedient to the calling God plants in us. We must keep in mind the worldwide
work of the body of Christ. The unborn are *so* important.
But they are not *more* important. Not more important than
the soul of the abortionist.

For God loves the victim *and* the victimizer!

That's a statement with the power to rattle us, isn't it? But
it's true. God loved the disciple Stephen. But as the crowd
was stoning him to death and Saul stood by nodding in approval, God loved Saul too. God knew Saul would one day
become the apostle Paul. We must remember that sin damns
us all but for the saving grace of God who loved the world.
No one, victim or victimizer, has more value than anyone
else, for each has eternal value in the sight of God.

And God calls different people to minister in this broken
world in a variety of ways. The prolife cause is not more
important than the other causes believers are called to. Some
are called to minister to AIDS victims, while others are called

to minister to the drug addicts who may have passed on AIDS to others. Some are called to minister to patients in hospitals, while others are called to minister to prisoners whose violence may have put those victims into the hospital. Some are called to work for justice in our judicial system, while others are called to come alongside murderers on death row.

Yes, God—in his great mercy—loves the victim *and* the victimizer. The unborn, the young mother in a crisis pregnancy, the mother's parent who insisted she abort her baby or be kicked out of her home, the abortion facility volunteer escort who assures the expectant mother she's making the right decision, the abortionist who kills the baby, the abortion worker who pieces together the aborted baby in the POC (products of conception) room, and the prolife prayer warrior praying outside the facility.

While visiting with tax collectors and sinners at the home of Matthew (a tax collector when Jesus called him), Jesus was challenged by the Pharisees for doing so. They asked, "Why does your teacher eat with tax collectors and sinners?" (Matt. 9:11).

In response, Jesus said this: "It is not the healthy who need a doctor, but the sick. But go and learn what this means: 'I desire mercy, not sacrifice.' For I have not come to call the righteous, but sinners" (Matt. 9:12–13).

I've taken his words, "Go and learn what this means: 'I desire mercy, not sacrifice,'" to heart. That's what this book is all about—my journey to understand and internalize mercy, and my sense of calling to share that mercy. The truth is, it's a challenge to understand God's mercy when it's given to those who anger, frustrate, or even dramatically differ from us. Mercy is not *our* nature—it is *God's* nature. I believe Jesus chose his words deliberately when he said to "go and learn." Mercy is a trait we must learn. And we must learn it by intentionally practicing it. One area where I've needed to practice God's mercy is when it comes to those who criticize my outreach to abortion workers. Another area for me is when it comes to those who don't take *some* kind of action for the cause of life. I need to grow in both respects.

The following verses from Ephesians 4 offer challenging and compelling insight and advice on how to grow in our mercy.

As a prisoner for the Lord, then, I urge you to live a life worthy of the calling you have received. Be completely humble and gentle; be patient, bearing with one another in love. Make every effort to keep the unity of the Spirit through the bond of peace. There is one body and one Spirit, just as you were called to one hope when you were called; one Lord, one faith, one baptism; one God and Father of all, who is over all and through all and in all. (vv. 1–6)

As you can see, humility, gentleness, patience, and bearing with one another in love are required of us. I don't know about you, but I confess here and now, none of these come easily to me. All take intentional practice—especially when I don't see eye to eye with someone. We are told to "make every effort" (v. 3). That's what it takes. Effort. We are to work at keeping the "unity of the Spirit" (v. 3).

Now read on.

So Christ himself gave the apostles, the prophets, the evangelists, the pastors and teachers, to equip his people for works of service, so that the body of Christ may be built up until we all reach unity in the faith and in the knowledge of the Son of God and become mature, attaining to the whole measure of the fullness of Christ. (vv. 11–13)

How fitting that this Scripture then goes on to list so many of the different gifts and roles that God has given us—each unique, each with its own priorities, each responding to a different set of needs. Some are called to reach out to nonbelievers or to victims or to victimizers, and some are called to build up believers. And how long are we to make this effort? God's Word is crystal clear: "Until we all reach unity in the faith and in the knowledge of the Son of God and become mature, attaining to the whole measure of the fullness of Christ" (v. 13). In other words, as long as we live on this earth. Is this a tall order? Yes, it is. But it's a worthy endeavor for those of us who long to become mature in our faith.

THE FOCUS FOR ME and my ministry was to be about the business of reaching out to abortion workers. I thought back to how prolifers had effectively reached out to me. Three things sprung to mind. One was their actions—standing in peaceful prayer day in and day out. Sure, I mocked them right along with my colleagues, but their consistency in acting on their beliefs made a powerful impression on me. Second was their manner—peaceful and kind. They greeted me with genuine warmth. They showed interest when I was pregnant. They spoke to me respectfully even when I blustered and threatened. The third thing that came to mind was a handwritten note mailed to me by Elizabeth, one of the faithful prayers at the fence. She had written: "The Lord has done great things for us, and we are filled with JOY!"

It was this third memory that stirred me. There is something personal and intimate about a handwritten note. It is evidence that someone took time and care to craft and send a message. When I first opened Elizabeth's note to me, it was disarming. I found it touching. To this day, I still carry that note in my wallet.

About that same time, a woman from a local church approached me with an idea. "You know, I love writing people cards. It's one of my love languages. I love encouraging people in that way," she said. She suggested that she and a small group of women at her church write letters for us. All we needed to do was purchase some stationery. They would even pay for the postage. That idea evolved. How might we at ATTWN use personal notes in an effective way to reach out to abortion workers? I believed we could.

Jennie and I got to work. We crafted several messages that we believed might appeal to an abortion worker who'd lost her zeal for her work in an abortion facility. Here is an example of one such message:

> We believe that you care for women. We believe that is why you were led to work where you do. We also believe that this job isn't what you thought it would be. We want you to know that we are here for you. You do NOT have to keep working here. You can quit, and we can help you by offering practical and financial assistance, help in finding a new job, and even a professional résumé writer who will help you look your best on paper so you can find a new job where you can truly use your passion for helping women. Please visit us at abortionworker.com. We are here for you. 888-570-5501. Our help is confidential.

We then designed a bright, appealing postcard, and the kind woman recruited a few volunteers to handwrite these notes—word for word, no variations—on the postcards.

Then we took on what was by far the most time-consuming, industrious endeavor. We began building an accurate database of every abortion facility in the United States. However, we didn't wait until the database was complete, knowing it would need work and maintenance for years to come. We got busy handwriting our postcards and mailing them to abortion facilities that we knew of.

Keep in mind, I worked in an abortion facility for eight years, so I wasn't naïve. I knew these postcards would get passed around these facilities and mocked by many abortion workers. The more attention they got, the more hands they passed through, the better. Sure, some might tear them up. Others might toss them in the trash. But I believed each card would plant a seed and send a message to someone—just the right someone—who might then respond. Maybe not the first time they saw one, but maybe the second or third time. Only God knew. We prayed our hearts out over these cards before we mailed them.

It worked! Not because it was some gimmick, but because the message was genuine. The words heartfelt.

Today, nearly a decade later, our handwritten postcards, which we send out two to three times a year, are still our most effective means of reaching out to abortion workers. Every single mailing elicits multiple responses.

There are two other primary ways abortion workers discover us. The second most frequent is that an abortion worker who has already discovered us and appreciated our services reaches out to another abortion worker they know and invites them to contact us. So often, as was true for me, there is a strong bond between coworkers in a facility. They care about women, and they care about one another, so when they receive genuine help, they want to share it with their friends.

The third most frequent method of discovery is that a pro-life sidewalk worker tells them about us. I love hearing that! It reminds me that just as I witnessed during my eight years in the abortion industry, there are good-hearted, faithful, and kind volunteers walking the sidewalks outside facilities and reaching out to abortion workers.

You may already be familiar with one such organization from my book *Unplanned*—40 Days for Life. Another organization that has my deep respect is Sidewalk Advocates for Life. Lauren Muzyka, who founded Sidewalk Advocates for Life, used to work for 40 Days for Life and had prayed in front of my clinic. Like me, she went to Texas A&M. She recognized the need for national sidewalk counseling training for those praying outside of abortion facilities and has led her organization in designing a highly effective four-hour training. I think it's the best training out there. They have 156 locations around the country (see https://sidewalkadvocates.org). One part of that training focuses completely on reaching out to the abortion worker, and I was honored to help design that section. It leaves their volunteers uniquely equipped to reach out to anyone going in and out of an abortion facility.

I have found that some people are a little skittish at the thought of talking to someone who works in an abortion clinic. Perhaps because the work they do is so abhorrent, or perhaps because it feels intimidating or threatening. Others ask, "How can you even pretend to love abortion workers or want to have a relationship with them?" My response is always the same: "If you're having to pretend, then you're not the right person for this outreach. It should be genuine, coming from your heart. This kind of outreach is a calling." I never have to pretend when I'm reaching out to these women—whether I'm on the sidewalk, on the other end of the phone, or responding online. God has planted in me a genuine desire to reach them. Just as those who reached out to me were called to do so and answered that call.

As you read on, I hope you are considering the ways in which God has gifted you and called you to demonstrate his mercy in a world that desperately needs it. And I hope you are stretched and challenged, as I still am, to "go and learn what this means: 'I desire mercy, not sacrifice'" (Matt. 9:13).

The next chapter explores one of the most audacious challenges God ever planted in my heart. It tested if I really believed that God loves both the victim and the victimizer and prompted me to put that belief into action. I pray it prompts you to perform audacious acts of mercy as well.

> He saved us, not because of righteous things we had done, but because of his mercy. He saved us through the washing of rebirth and renewal by the Holy Spirit.
>
> Titus 3:5

6

THE MIRROR

By May 2013, as Jennie and I approached the one-year anniversary of And Then There Were None, we were deeply grateful that God had used our ministry to ensure that there were now fifty-six fewer abortion workers in the abortion industry. And we could see that the need for ATTWN wasn't slowing down; it was accelerating.

But our "quitters," as we affectionately called them, weren't the only ones who'd left the industry. There were others—some notorious—who'd been forced out of it. The eyes of the world that month were riveted to news about the outcome of the Kermit Gosnell trial. I'd been following the trial closely since its beginning in March, and on May 13, 2013, I was holding my breath for the verdict.

Here's the background as it was reported in *The Atlantic*:

On February 18, 2010, the FBI raided the "Women's Medical Society," entering its offices about 8:30 p.m. Agents expected to find evidence that it was illegally selling prescription drugs.

On entering, they quickly realized something else was amiss. In the grand jury report's telling, "There was blood on the floor. A stench of urine filled the air. A flea-infested cat was wandering through the facility, and there were cat feces on the stairs. Semi-conscious women scheduled for abortions were moaning in the waiting room or the recovery room, where they sat on dirty recliners covered with blood-stained blankets. All the women had been sedated by unlicensed staff." Authorities had also learned about the patient that died at the facility several months prior.[1]

The public health officials who examined the facility also discovered the following horrific findings:

- Unsterilized instruments
- Rusty, outdated equipment
- Poorly maintained oxygen equipment
- Fetal remains stored "haphazardly" throughout the clinic—"in bags, milk jugs, orange juice cartons, and even in cat-food containers"[2]
- Lack of functioning resuscitation or monitoring equipment—except for *one* blood pressure cuff

Gosnell acknowledged to the investigating detective that at least 10 percent of the fetuses aborted at the facility had been older than twenty-four weeks in gestation—the upper legal limit for abortions in Pennsylvania. The grand jury report noted,

When you perform late-term "abortions" by inducing labor, you get babies. Live, breathing, squirming babies. By 24 weeks, most babies born prematurely will survive if they receive appropriate medical care. But that was not what the Women's Medical Society was about. Gosnell had a simple solution for the unwanted babies he delivered: he killed them. He didn't call it that. He called it "ensuring fetal demise." The way he ensured fetal demise was by sticking scissors into the back of the baby's neck and cutting the spinal cord. He called that "snipping." . . .

All the employees of the Women's Medical Society . . . acted as if it wasn't murder at all. Most of these acts cannot be prosecuted because Gosnell destroyed the files. Among the relatively few cases that could be specifically documented, one was Baby Boy A. His 17-year-old mother was almost 30 weeks pregnant—seven and a half months—when labor was induced. An employee estimated his birth weight as approaching six pounds. He was breathing and moving when Gosnell severed his spine and put the body in a plastic shoebox for disposal. The doctor joked that this baby was so big he could "walk me to the bus stop." Another, Baby Boy B, whose body was found at the clinic frozen in a one-gallon spring-water bottle, was at least 28 weeks of gestational age when he was killed. Baby C was moving and breathing for 20 minutes before an assistant came in and cut the spinal cord, just the way she had seen Gosnell do it so many times. And these were not even the worst cases.[3]

After the FBI raid on the Women's Medical Society, Gosnell's license to practice medicine was suspended. "The Department of Health filed papers to start the process of closing the clinic. The district attorney submitted the case to the grand jury on May 4, 2010."[4] Gosnell and nine of his staff, including his wife, Pearl, were arrested and charged in January 2011 with a wide variety of offenses, including, in some cases, murder. Since then, they had been awaiting trial.

Many who had known Gosnell in the early years of his medical career were surprised to learn that he was running a facility like this. He had been practicing for decades and started out as a community physician who went on house calls. At that point in his career, he was respected in the community as a reputable physician. An African American, he worked with low-income people and minorities, which led many to see him as very generous. And yet the details of what went on in his abortion facility in Philadelphia turned America's stomach.

Finally, the verdict was in. On May 13, 2013, Gosnell was convicted of three counts of murder, one count of involuntary manslaughter, and over two hundred lesser counts. The next day he struck a deal with the prosecution to waive his rights to appeal in return for a sentence of life in prison without possibility of parole. Four of his staff were either convicted of or pled guilty to murder; the rest were convicted of or pled guilty to lesser charges.

Horrific? Yes. Hard to forgive? Undoubtedly.

But God doesn't ask us to do just the easy stuff.

THERE WAS A REASON I awaited the sentencing with such intense interest. This case was personal to me. More than personal. I felt connected to Gosnell and his staffers, and for a very good reason—I'd been praying daily for them, by name, since the story first broke in May 2010. Three years. I'd also been writing to them, individually, since their January 2011 arrests. Their case first hit the news only six months after my own dramatic turn from pro-choice to prolife. I was still raw with emotion, my newfound spiritual life was on fire, and my conscience was in its early days of being awakened.

These people were charged with the most heinous crimes against the weakest, most vulnerable members of society. But I also knew that I was no better and no different. At Planned Parenthood, we killed babies through suction, but that was a distinction without a difference—we weren't any better than Gosnell. Please understand that I'm not making excuses for Gosnell and his team. It's just that, because of my background, I had a heart for those people who went to prison because of this case—even Gosnell himself. I believe he started out with good intentions—helping people. But somewhere along the course of his life, sin snuck in. Did it tiptoe in as greed? Ambition? Who but God knows? But however he was tempted, he gave in, and that sin changed his heart. I knew how easily that could happen because it happened to me.

As horrible as it sounds, looking at Kermit Gosnell and what he did was like looking in a mirror. I looked at him, but I saw my own reflection, my sins as black and repugnant as his.

I imagined Gosnell's staff in their cells, and I thought, *There but for the grace and mercy of God go I.*

The content of my letters to them was simple. I wanted them to know that I cared about them. I wanted them to know that since leaving the abortion industry, I had become a prolife activist and I understood how easily, working in that environment, they could begin to feel trapped, to feel manipulated into staying in that world even if they didn't want to. And I wasn't alone in this—my dear friend Kris wrote and prayed right along with me. We would pray over every letter we sent, and we prayed for each one of them, including Kermit Gosnell, by name, every single day. (I can't wait until you get to chapter 8 and discover one of the ways God answered those prayers!)

When I was confirmed as a Catholic, I chose Mary Magdalene as my confirmation saint. I felt an immediate connection to her. She had sinned so much and been forgiven in even greater amounts. She knew she didn't deserve forgiveness, but she received it anyway. And because of this, she clung to Christ. She knew she was nothing without him.

Like Mary Magdalene, I've committed my share of sins, including betraying the trust of the women who came to Planned Parenthood in the worst possible way: I convinced them to kill their children. And that made me an accomplice to murder, not once but thousands of times. Women came to me expecting accurate information, and instead I lied to them. I was among the worst sinners, those who help to destroy life. I'm no better than Kermit Gosnell, and it would be arrogant and dishonest of me to think I am.

Besides that, I ended the life of my own children, twice. Not because I was coerced or didn't know better. It was because I thought children would be an inconvenience to my lifestyle. I am responsible for their deaths; no one else.

But despite the depravity of all those sins, I, like Mary Magdalene, have been forgiven even though I didn't deserve that forgiveness.

So, when I hear someone say things like, "Murderers and people like Kermit Gosnell don't deserve to breathe the same air as I do—I hope he burns in hell," it hurts. Because I could be described in the same way. And not just me. I know that words like those hurt others who have left the abortion industry—people who work every day to not only recover from their sins but also somehow make reparation for them.

Words like that also hurt people who are still in the industry and, hearing those words, think they will be shunned by the prolife movement if they take the step I and many others have taken and leave the industry. I've been told by several former abortion workers that they will *never* come forward with their stories because they're so scared of how they will be treated by the prolife world. I wish I could say their fears are unfounded, but, in fact, they are legitimate.

Yes, I repented and came out of the world of abortion. But what if I hadn't *yet*? Imagine me still at Planned Parenthood a year before I was dumbstruck by that ultrasound that changed the course of my life—my "Damascus Road" moment. Even if you were justified at that point in saying I was an accomplice to murder, even if there'd been a certain moral truth in saying I deserved to die—remember that I wasn't brought out of the abortion industry by angry voices accusing me of my sins. I was loved out of the movement by prolifers who'd been praying for and speaking lovingly to me for years. When God brought my sins before my eyes and I could no longer bear to continue in them, I ran first to those same loving prolifers. Could I have done that if their voices had been angry and accusing all those years?

And remember, too, that God could have called me in to help with a similar ultrasound at any earlier point, but he did not; he chose the timing. And his timing is perfect. Are we really willing to say that repentance is all about us—about us being good enough or wise enough to change our direction? Certainly not. Repentance comes about through the urging of the Holy Spirit in God's perfect time. Many of those still in the movement simply haven't repented *yet*—because their moment of God's fierce mercy hasn't come.

The people I turned to after my Damascus Road moment accepted me as I was, baggage and all. They knew I was a broken person, but they extended their love to me anyway. They knew I needed significant healing, and they even helped provide it.

One story always makes me tear up. Karen, one of the prolife women who immediately befriended me after I left Planned Parenthood, was asked by a reporter, "What was Abby like before she became prolife? How nasty was she?"

Karen's genuine, Christlike response was simply, "I don't remember that person. She is a new creation in Christ. I won't talk about her past. I only want to talk about her future."

What grace! What forgiveness! She undoubtedly knew lots of stories about my impulsive and unloving words and actions, but she chose not to repeat them. Why? Because she truly loved me—and she always had, even while I was working at Planned Parenthood. She always believed my conversion would happen.

It was Christ who changed me, along with the merciful and compassionate words of his people. It wasn't the condemnation of those who yelled and called me names. It was the words of people like Karen—those who prayed that I would one day walk out of that clinic and never go back. I am here because of them and their Christlike witness.

Don't we want that for every abortion clinic worker and abortion provider? Don't we want that for Kermit Gosnell? I smile every time I imagine his conversion. What a heavenly victory that will be! Can it happen? If you say no—just remember that God is in the business of miracles. My God doesn't want anyone to suffer in hell. He wants *all* his children to come to him. And yes, that includes us "monsters" who are in or have been in the abortion industry.

Mercy comes from Christ—and hate comes from hell. When we have hate in our hearts, that's an indication that our spirits are damaged. Make sure that you, as a living witness of Christ and his truth, and your words reflect Christ's mercy and not hate. Otherwise, you could be putting your own soul at risk. "Anyone who hates a brother or sister is a murderer, and you know that no murderer has eternal life residing in him" (1 John 3:15). When we hate, we are no better than those who kill.

Anyone who knows me can tell you that Abby Johnson is not the world's sweetest person. If you're looking for someone who lives out the notion that you catch more flies with honey than vinegar, don't look here. Sometimes I'm all vinegar. What do you expect? I worked for years in the abortion industry—could a tenderhearted person have done that?

Most former abortion industry workers like me aren't like you. We may not be the most kindhearted. Maybe you don't understand how we could have done what we did. But once we leave that industry—we are fighters. We are fierce. We are passionate. We don't waste time beating around the bush, not when it comes to life, especially the lives that we helped take. We acknowledge the sins of our past, and we're willing to take hits for them. We are willing to stand up and be counted even in places where no one else is standing, places that make us (and would make you too) uncomfortable. Why are we willing to take those bruises, bruises that sometimes come from those who should be rejoicing at our repentance? We know that we have to, because of our past.

It's the price we must pay.

Those of us who have worked in the industry live with a constant burden, one that we will not be freed from until we reach heaven. And that burden, as uncomfortable as it is, is what keeps us burning for justice. It reminds us why we fight so hard. We have seen death and evil in a way that most haven't. We were, in fact, active participants.

But now we are forgiven.

And those who have been forgiven much, love much. So, we have a lot of love to give.

Near the start of this chapter, I wrote about the evils perpetrated in the abortion mill owned and operated by Kermit Gosnell. Yes, those evils were unacceptable, unfathomable, unspeakable. And yes, he was responsible for every one of them. Yet I felt called to take the time to write to him in prison and to pray for him daily. I'm still at it. God's mercy toward me was fierce and irresistible, and I must offer that same mercy toward others, no matter how repugnant their sins.

That's why I am eagerly awaiting the day I can call Kermit Gosnell a *former* and *repentant* abortion provider.

Even though I was once a blasphemer and a persecutor and a violent man, I was shown mercy.

1 Timothy 1:13

7

"WHOSE CHOICE? YOUR CHOICE"

On June 20, 2013, my son Luke was born.

Five days later, I bundled up my baby and headed for the Texas State Capitol in Austin. On the side of Luke's infant carrier, I had written "Abortion is mean." Grace, six, and Alex, eleven months, were home with Doug, who was still loving being a stay-at-home dad.

June 25, 2013, wasn't just a "business as usual" day at the Texas State Capitol. The Texas legislature had been debating a bill that was considered crucial by prolifers and a threat by abortion supporters. SB5—Senate Bill 5—contained several measures that would affect the ability of providers to perform abortions. The bill would do the following:

1. Ban abortions after twenty weeks post-fertilization.
2. Require doctors who perform abortions to have admitting privileges at a hospital no more than thirty miles away.

3. Require abortion clinics to meet the same standards as other surgical health-care facilities in the state.

4. Require that women taking abortion-inducing drugs, such as RU-486, receive medical oversight.

5. Not apply to abortions necessary to save a pregnant woman's life or prevent permanent bodily damage from a pregnancy.

June 25 was the final day of the special session of the legislature called to debate the bill, and I felt compelled to be there. What I had *hoped* would happen was that the debate over the bill would end, a vote would be called, and the bill would pass. But despite my hopes, I was aware that the bill's opponents would try to defeat it by any means necessary.

The crowd packing all public areas of the capitol consisted of both supporters and opponents of the bill. Both sides were equally vocal and equally committed. But who can resist a cute baby? So, as I passed through the crowd with Luke in his stroller, I heard from prolifers and abortion supporters alike.

"He is so adorable!"

"What a precious gift."

"What a beautiful baby!"

At first I responded to their compliments with, "Thank you." But eventually—maybe it was hormones or the sheer irony of the pro-choicers' comments as they gathered to defeat a bill because it would make it harder to abort babies just like Luke—I couldn't take it anymore. Accuse me of politicizing my baby son if you want to, but I began to respond to their compliments with, "Yes, he is beautiful. And just five days ago, it would have been legal to kill him by abortion. Which is what you are here to support."

I got no return comments from any of the women—just blank stares.

I entered the Senate's gallery while Democratic Senator Wendy Davis and some of her colleagues were attempting a filibuster to defeat the bill. And I knew the filibuster might succeed—after all, the session, by law, ended at midnight. How long could she keep it up? I listened to her pro-choice rhetoric. It was hard not to stand up and yell out the truth.

I was truly amazed. This woman clearly knew nothing about the reality of Planned Parenthood. It sounded as if she had bought every lie they throw to the public. It was saddening to think that in order to ensure that women in Texas would have easy access to kill their children, Senator Davis was willing to experience such discomfort—no breaks of any kind, including for the bathroom (which meant she took the stage outfitted with a catheter), no food, and no water. In the end, she had stood there for eleven hours.

A vote was called that night, but Davis's attempt to delay the vote had been successful: The vote came two minutes too late. SB5 had been defeated. Now it was up to Governor Rick Perry to make a decision—and he did have a few options that would keep the bill alive.

The next day, June 26, Governor Perry announced a second special session of the legislature to consider some things that he saw as priorities—including this bill, which would be kept alive by reintroducing it in a slightly altered form as HB2—House Bill 2. We prolifers weren't surprised, but we also knew we had our work cut out for us. We worked to rally even more troops for our side. Still, we were confident. We knew we had the votes.

Talking points were written and distributed to prolife groups. Special temporary Facebook groups were created to keep everyone informed and efforts coordinated. People were excited. We knew this wasn't just politics. This was a spiritual battle, and we were armed with prayer.

On July 1, the second special session began. Prolifers showed up in droves to support passage of the bill, but on that day, for some reason, hardly any abortion supporters were at the capitol yet. We knew, though, that they were coming.

Texas already had some tough abortion laws. Two years before, in 2011, HB15, informally known as the "sonogram law," had passed and been signed into law. It requires that any woman attempting to get an abortion in Texas has to have a sonogram—an ultrasound—within twenty-four hours before the abortion procedure. The doctor who does the sonogram must be the same doctor who performs the abortion, and they must display the sonogram images to the pregnant woman, explain the results, and play the heartbeat audibly. The law also requires that the doctor describe to the pregnant woman the medical risks of an abortion and determine the gestational age of the fetus. In 2012, that law was challenged by pro-choice groups and upheld by the US Court of Appeals for the Fifth Circuit, as well as by a US Supreme Court decision about a similar North Carolina law. Yes, we had some good laws limiting abortion, but we needed more. We needed this law.

My life had been a bit hectic in the previous weeks. Since June 25, I'd been at the capitol most days. There would be no time off anytime soon, either, because now the campaign to support this bill would begin in earnest.

It was a circus. A colorful circus too. I don't remember whose idea it was, but someone suggested that all of us there to support passage of the bill wear blue. And we did. The opponents of the bill saw that and decided that they, too, would have a defining color, and theirs was orange. To anybody who didn't know what was going on, it must have looked like a convention of Denver Broncos fans!

Some days were relatively quiet—business as usual, seeing if you can get some time with someone to express your support for the bill, which is the kind of thing you do when you're lobbying. Other days, prolife rallies were held inside the capitol. The pro-choice side attempted to disrupt those rallies however they could, so the rotunda was filled mostly with women in orange screaming that we were taking their rights and forcing our religious beliefs on them. There's also an open-air rotunda, or central court, and the prolife side planned an event there to give women who'd had abortions a chance to tell their own abortion story—including their regrets and misgivings. It was livestreamed.

The pro-choice side "invaded" that event in some of the most bizarre ways. For instance, one group was yelling, "Hail, Satan!" Others were screaming nearby, trying to make as much noise as possible to disrupt the event. Of course, they waved signs—and so did we. But some of their signs were vulgar and profane. Some of the prolife women had brought their older children so they could see how government works—how in this country we can make our voices heard by lawmakers. The pro-choicers were yelling profanity into those children's faces. They had also come with supplies designed to wreak havoc among the prolife group, and they used them. They threw used tampons. They hurled jars of feces.

I recoiled in shock. I'd once been a pro-choice demonstrator who'd stood proudly shoulder to shoulder with other pro-choicers lobbying for abortion rights. I remembered the feeling of seeing myself as a champion of women's rights, aligned with my sisters in the cause, but never had I seen pro-choicers so rabid in their anger, spewing spit and obscenities from their mouths. In all the years I spent at Planned Parenthood, in all the rallies I went to either in support of or in opposition to abortion, I had never seen anything so deplorable.

Since leaving Planned Parenthood, when I had looked back on the years I spent as part of that organization, I had felt regret. I had felt remorse. But that night at the Texas State Capitol, I felt something I had never felt before about my years with Planned Parenthood: embarrassment. When I saw how those women supporting abortion were behaving, I was so embarrassed that I had ever been a part of this group, even though personally I never acted like that.

It was a bizarre scene, and frankly, it felt dangerous at times because it was an angry mob. Not that there wasn't plenty of security. The state had pulled state troopers from all over the state to come to the capitol. There was a large, visible presence of law enforcement.

The self-control of the prolifers in the face of that vitriol was amazing. Pro-choicers were yelling in our faces, spitting on people, even pushing people around, and yet I never saw any prolifer retaliate.

On July 10, the day the House was expected to vote on the bill, emotions on both sides were at fever pitch. Inside the capitol rotunda stood a Black woman, dressed in blue. She lifted her prolife sign smack-dab in the middle of the rotunda, surrounded closely by what seemed like thousands of pro-choicers. The orange-clad group was screaming and chanting, swinging their bras over their heads. I wish I could remember what the prolife woman's sign said. What I do remember, clearly, is that as she stood there completely out-numbered amid the aggressive attitudes of the pro-choice crowd, she appeared to be singing. But there was far too much noise in that space that day for me to make out the words to her song.

I thought, *I have to go down there. She shouldn't have to face this alone.* So, I made my way through the crowd. It was a raucous and bizarre scene—women in orange shirts screaming at the top of their lungs, some of them still throwing tampons.

Not until I got within a few feet of her could I hear her song. It was "Amazing Grace." I grabbed her hand and stood with her. I couldn't even sing along because I was so overwhelmed by all that was happening around us. I closed my eyes. The protesters in orange were so close I could feel their breath on my neck as they yelled, "Whose choice? My choice!"

Other prolifers saw us and came over to join. Within a few minutes, more than a dozen of us were huddled together in the middle of the rotunda, surrounded by orange shirts. As I looked up at the three levels of gallery above, I could see three stories of orange T-shirts and tank tops, all screaming hate. I was so overwhelmed, I started to cry. *What have we come to*, I thought, *that there are people this angry at us simply because we are trying to protect the unborn?*

The chants of the pro-choicers died away gradually as they began to file out for a planned outdoor rally. I scanned the crowd as they left, and suddenly I saw, not far from me on the rotunda floor, somebody I used to work with at Planned Parenthood. We locked eyes, and for a moment it was as if I'd forgotten that we were now on different sides of the fence. I was happy to see this woman with whom I'd been friends for years while we both worked at the clinic, so I smiled and waved. "Hey," I mouthed.

She pointed at me, eyes full of hate, and mouthed, very clearly, a foul word. That was all she said. Then she turned and walked outside to join the rally.

It was a quick and unmistakable reminder: This wasn't a reunion with an old friend. We were each firmly settled into opposing positions on one of the most inflammatory issues facing the country. We were not on the same side. Our eight-year friendship was over, regardless of how much I wished it wasn't. And that was not because of who I was but rather because of whom I now defended.

As stunning and saddening as that exchange was, I remained standing there for a while in the middle of the rotunda. I *needed* to be in the middle. I had to feel that heaviness. I can too easily forget what this darkness feels like. I need to be reminded from time to time of why I fight so hard and what we are truly up against.

While the women dressed in blue clashed with those in orange in the rotunda, the members of the Texas House of Representatives were in their chamber in the west wing of the capitol completing their debates, defense, and attacks of HB2 as they prepared to vote.

The capitol has a basement and then an extension that includes two underground floors packed with offices. One of the state legislators had handed over one of those underground offices to some of us who were leaders among the prolifers in attendance. When I left the rotunda, I headed to the office to join several others. Even there, below ground, we could hear the roaring of the pro-choice group when they finished their rally outside and began, noisily, to reenter the rotunda—which was far removed from where we were in the extension.

I began to get texts from friends still outside the capitol stating that the state troopers weren't allowing them to move through the pro-choice crowd to get to us. I tried texting my friends directions on how to get around the rotunda through different stairwells and back hallways. I had discovered these get-arounds over the years I'd been promoting prolife legislation at the capitol. But the state troopers blocked them at every turn, trying to keep the prolife people and the pro-choice crowd separated. They feared that in the heat of the moment someone from one side would attack someone from the other. We decided everyone was safest just staying where they were, so we locked the door and settled in.

We had a TV in the office, and we had it set to watch a livestream of what was happening upstairs in the House Chamber. We sat, silent and tense, at the edges of our seats, riveted to every word.

And then it was time for the vote. We watched with growing excitement as the votes were tallied—and it takes a long time to tally 145 votes. We knew we had the votes and didn't expect any unpleasant surprises, but still, it isn't over till it's over. And when the passage of the bill was announced, ninety-six votes to forty-nine, we had a huge celebration there among those of us crowded into that underground office—lots of hugging, lots of cheering, even some tears of joy. We had worked so hard to get this passed that now we were giddy, acting like kids.

The celebration tapered off after a while and there was a pause—and then it hit all of us that we needed to get out of there. We feared a riot or violence might erupt. When we opened the door into the hallway, we could hear pro-choicers singing the song "We're Not Gonna Take It" by Twisted Sister. We had heard reports of a man carrying a gun around the capitol steps. True? We didn't know, but this was Texas, after all, where some people carry guns out in the open routinely, so to err on the side of caution, we wanted to get out of the capitol quickly, and that's what we did.

The bill had passed the House, but it still had to pass the Senate. Over the next three days, the bill made its way to a final vote in the Texas Senate . . . and, as we had expected, it passed. All that remained was for Governor Perry to sign the bill. Five days later, on July 18, 2013, he did.

Texas had now passed the most restrictive prolife legislation in the country, but it hadn't been without opposition. Throughout the bill's frustrating journey through the Texas legislature, abortion supporters had made themselves heard. They had come loudly with their attitude and vulgar signs and profane language. They had handcuffed themselves to railings. It had, indeed, been a spectacle. They were full of anger and hate, but beneath it all, I could not allow myself to forget that they were also full of pain.

No doubt they thought their loud and profane demonstration was brilliant. But then their minds are no longer solely their own. Their free will remains. But with every evil act—every *sin*—a person commits, the evil hooks itself deeper and deeper into them, until their thoughts, words, and behavior are heavily influenced by it.

And I'm an example of that. When I look back to my time with Planned Parenthood, I can't believe some of the things that came out of my mouth. Lies that I knew were lies at the time. It's as if I was a different person. And in a way, I *was* a different person.

We can't afford to become consumed by hate and contempt toward anyone, so we must pray that misguided individuals one day become new creations in Christ. That's what I pray for my former friend, the one I saw in the capitol rotunda. That's what I pray for all clinic workers. It's what I pray for women who have chosen abortion. It's what I pray for those people who stood around me in the rotunda, screaming in my ears and staring at me with disdain as I stood with my friend who was singing "Amazing Grace." I pray because I know it works.

I had never been prouder to be prolife than on those long days at the Texas State Capitol in the summer of 2013. We showed up and made a difference. We put up a fight—a holy fight—for Christ and his truth. We were united for one cause. We were compassionate. We were slow to anger. We were kind. We were merciful. We were prayerful. We were exactly what Christ intended us to be. And now, we are being rewarded. Abortion facilities quickly began closing. In 2011, there were forty-four clinics in Texas that performed abortions. In 2021, there were twenty-two.

Today, as I write about the pivotal role played by prolifers in this historic Texas legislation, I think about the chant of the pro-choicers that day: *Whose choice? My choice!* There is a lot of truth in that, but not the truth they intended.

We all have choices to make when it comes to playing a role in demonstrating God's mercy to this often brutal, merciless world. And we all have choices regarding the way we play our role. As you stand overlooking the chaotic clash between good and evil in your world, what choices will you make? Will you stay home and watch it on a screen? Will you step out and take your place in the balcony? Maybe you will venture out into the danger zone and lift your voice, singing "Amazing Grace" no matter the chanting that surrounds you—or stand alongside others leading in that way, despite your fear.

I appeal to you, today, to remember that you have a choice. Make one. Whose choice? *Your choice!*

AFTER MY CONVERSION to prolife but while I still lived in College Station, I would often go to the Planned Parenthood clinic in Bryan to kneel outside the fence and pray—for the women who were coming there for abortions and for the women, many of whom I had once counted as friends, who worked there. After I moved to Austin, I didn't have much contact with the clinic anymore.

So, one day in June 2013, I called the clinic from my home office, just to keep tabs on them. When Texas passed the sonogram bill in 2011, I knew it would really hurt the clinic's ability to offer abortions. I was just checking—were they still able to offer abortions? If so, how often?

"I'm sorry," the receptionist said. "We're not able to provide abortions at this time because of what happened with the sonogram bill that passed a couple of years ago."

The bill, as I've mentioned, required that a physician be present at the clinic two days in a row if they were going to perform abortions—the first day to give the sonogram and the second to perform the abortion. The Bryan clinic had a doctor who came from out of town only one day a week—and he wasn't able to come more often because he had a full-time job elsewhere.

The receptionist sounded apologetic. "But if you can get to Houston," she said, "our clinic there can help you."

"No, that's okay. Thank you," I said, and hung up. Then I pumped my fist and said, "Yes!" What a surge of gratitude and joy I felt when I heard her say that, just as we'd hoped, the law that made it difficult for clinics in smaller cities to continue to perform abortions had shut down abortions in my old clinic! So exciting.

And by the way, that ultrasound (or sonogram) requirement applies to abortions performed via drugs, such as RU-486, as well as through surgical means. We knew providers weren't just switching clients over to chemical abortions—first, because that, too, would violate the new law, and second, because all abortions have to be reported, including chemical abortions, and all the reports of abortion numbers in Texas were trending steadily down.

After I hung up that day, I just sat for a couple of minutes, reveling in the realization of something long sought coming to pass. *Oh my word*, I thought. *Oh my word, oh my word, oh my word! This is really happening!* The Bryan clinic was not providing abortions anymore. And I had a sudden thought: *within six months, they'll be closed.*

That night when I told Doug that the clinic was no longer providing abortions, his first question was this: "How long do you think it'll be before they shut down?"

"Has to be within six months," I said, "because financially they can't survive without the dollars they make from abortions."

ON JULY 18, 2013, Governor Perry signed HB2 into law. I was at the capitol for it, along with a lot of other prolife leaders. We couldn't miss that big day. We were actually present for the signing, and then the governor posed for pictures with each of us.

Along with several friends, I headed for the capitol cafeteria, where I sat distractedly scrolling through my email but with my mind mostly on what I'd just experienced and the exhilaration of having the bill now officially the law in Texas. Then something on my phone caught my eye: a press release from Planned Parenthood.

I opened it up. I first skimmed it and then, in disbelief, went back to read it more carefully to make sure it said what I thought it said. And then I began repeating, just as I had not long ago after that phone call with the Bryan clinic, "Oh my word! Oh my word! Oh my word!"

The people sitting with me asked, "What? Tell us."

I couldn't even say it out loud. I didn't believe it. I read through the press release one more time as carefully as I could in my overexcited state. And finally, I said, "The Bryan Planned Parenthood clinic is closing."

Shocked silence. They couldn't believe it either. And then they all spoke at once.

"Are you serious?"

"How do you know?"

"Are you sure it's not a scam?"

"I'm looking at the press release from Planned Parenthood," I said. "They're closing. Not just my old clinic in Bryan but also two more: Huntsville and Lufkin."

The press release didn't credit the new abortion restrictions with causing the closings. In fact, it specifically said the closings had nothing to do with abortion. Instead, it said funding cuts to the state women's health program that the Texas legislature had passed a couple of years before were the main cause. But I knew from firsthand experience how crucial those dollars from abortion were to Planned Parenthood's financial health and that the new law had a great deal to do with the closing of the three clinics.

I WROTE ABOUT the closing of my former clinic in the epilogue of the updated 2014 edition of *Unplanned* (it was also portrayed in the movie based on that book), so perhaps it seems unnecessary to include it here. But it was such a major development, not only for me but for the prolife movement in Texas, that I can't resist. I'll limit myself to the most significant memories, at least for me.

- When I tried to grasp the importance of the closing of 4112 E. 29th St., Bryan, Texas, the clinic I'd directed for Planned Parenthood for years, I thought first of all those prolifers who'd prayed faithfully outside the fence and who had, despite our wide difference in beliefs, befriended me. People like Marilisa Carney, who had, beyond all logic or reason, reached out to me and made me feel valued on my very first day working at the clinic. Sister Marie Bernadette, kneeling in her full nun habit on the sidewalk in the Texas summer heat, tears running down her face for the lives being lost. Mr. Orozco, faithfully praying outside the fence twice a week for almost fifteen years. Bobby Reynoso, praying on his knees with his arms uplifted in praise on the day I resigned and drove out of the parking lot. And so many others. Would this have happened without their faithful prayers?

- Would ATTWN have been created without the overwhelmingly supportive response to the first edition of *Unplanned*? Without Shawn Carney's words on that October day when I fled the clinic and sought out him and his staff at their office (to their amazement!): "Abby, we've always told you we were here to help. We'll help you or anyone at the clinic who wants to leave. We're going to help you get out."

- What a thrill it was when the clinic shut its doors for the final time (as a Planned Parenthood clinic, at least) on August 1, 2013! And just a few weeks later, on September 7, all of us who'd had anything to do with protesting abortion at the clinic rejoiced at a moving celebration ceremony.

- At that celebration, I took two roses, one red in memory of my own aborted child years before through that facility, and one white in memory of the thousands of unborn who had died within the walls of that building. Overcome with grief, I threaded their stems through the lattice of the fence where the faithful had prayed for so many years. Yes, it was a day to mourn, and I did. But it was also a day to celebrate. And on that day in 2013, I didn't even yet know that that building would shortly become the headquarters of 40 Days for Life, where campaigns to combat abortion would be planned and carried out for years to come!

As I've said before, my healing and my grieving have tended to be public rather than private. As I prayed on the sidewalk that day, kneeling next to my two roses, there were cameras clicking and flashes going off and media recording the details. Very public. And if you think that made me believe my attitudes, words, and actions needed to be a model of humility and mercy for those present that day and those who would hear the news reports and see the photos and videos in the media, you'd be right. But even though I was aware that I was on display, the humility came naturally. As excited as I was about the clinic closing, it was not my triumph—it was God's. None of this had happened through my own efforts—I am too puny, too ineffective. God had made it happen, and God deserved all the credit. Just as all love is an expression of God's love, made possible by his overwhelming love for us, all mercy is an outpouring of God's mercy.

> Therefore, since through God's mercy we have this ministry, we do not lose heart.
>
> 2 Corinthians 4:1

8

THE LENS OF MERCY

I t was no surprise to Adrienne Moton of Philadelphia when she heard the knock at her door and realized it was the police. And she knew exactly why they were there. "Adrienne Moton, you're under arrest. You have the right to remain silent. Anything you say can and will be used against you . . ."

Robbery? Drug charges? No. Adrienne had worked for years at Kermit Gosnell's abortion clinic. And she knew that, regardless of her opinions (or anyone else's) about legal abortion, many of the abortions she had participated in at the clinic had not been legal because of the fetus's advanced gestational age. In fact, those abortions had amounted to murder. She'd had no doubt for some time that she would be arrested and charged with those murders.

Her employment at Gosnell's clinic had started informally years before. In fact, she'd known Kermit Gosnell and his wife, Pearl, long before she started working there. They were family friends. Growing up, she'd called him Uncle Kermit. She'd even lived with the Gosnells for a while as a teenager because of problems at home. When Adrienne had her first unplanned pregnancy, Uncle Kermit offered to take care of it for free, just as a favor.

It's important to understand the relationship Adrienne had with Kermit Gosnell. By the time he asked her to volunteer at the clinic, she already had him on a pedestal. After all, he had helped her when she was down and vulnerable. And she was so young and inexperienced and trusting that when he said, "This is what we do with these fetuses," she just went along with it, not questioning the morality. After all, this was Uncle Kermit.

At first, he assigned her to clean the instruments used in abortions. Then, when she was in her twenties, he offered to take her on as a regular paid employee—at the modest wage of ten dollars an hour, in cash, paid off the books.

Like many of us who have worked in the industry, despite her lack of medical training, Adrienne was entrusted to do things she shouldn't have been doing—performing ultrasounds, administering medication, helping with abortions, and disposing of fetal remains. At the time, she didn't *know* she shouldn't be doing those things, because her employer had never trained her on what is called scope of practice—what's legal or appropriate. In such circumstances, it's easy to tell yourself, *The people I work with are medically trained nurses and doctors. They surely wouldn't mislead me on what's okay for me to do here.* And that makes complete sense. The problem is that sometimes this doesn't turn out to be true. Some unethical abortion facilities don't give their employees reliable information about the applicable laws.

I know what you're thinking: *How could that be true? Don't they want the best-trained, best-informed, best-qualified people they can afford to hire?* I wish that were true of all facilities. But let me tell you about an abortion worker (I will call her Luanne), who came to us through And Then There Were None. She was an RN. She needed a job and was hired by a well-known abortion provider in her state. The total duration of her employment there was twenty-three days.

Luanne was dedicated to the integrity of her profession and the well-being of her patients, and as soon as she saw what was happening at the facility—the lack of care, the lack of protocols—she quit. She became a whistleblower and talked to regulators in her state, exposing what was going on at that particular facility, which the state ended up temporarily closing. And why did that happen? Because the provider had hired a qualified, competent nurse who wouldn't tolerate unethical actions that could harm patients.

Over the time Adrienne worked at Kermit Gosnell's clinic, many odd and frightening things caught her attention and made her uneasy, including the following:

- Gosnell would take photos of women's genitalia and mount them in a series of photo books. He was using them for research, he said, yet he never published anything related to those photos.
- So many babies were far over the legal gestational age limit—twenty-four weeks in Pennsylvania—for abortion. Adrienne took a picture of one that was thirty weeks in gestational age that had been delivered and then killed.
- *Shouldn't medical facilities be spotlessly clean?* she asked herself—and yet Gosnell's clinic was filthy and unsterile, with a pet cat that left feces in the stairwell.

- Adrienne watched women walk out with prescriptions for highly addictive painkillers—a higher quantity and much more powerful than necessary. She knew a pill mill when she saw one.

Eventually it became too much. *I just can't do this anymore*, she thought. *We're lying about the gestational ages. Killing viable babies with a pair of scissors? No, I'm done.* So, she quit in 2008.

Adrienne had already left the clinic before that fateful day in 2009 when Karnamaya Mongar, an immigrant from Bhutan who had come in for an abortion, died on the table, but she heard about it from her coworkers. "When I heard that, I knew exactly what happened," she said. "I was sure that someone had overdosed her. There was no protocol, so they would just keep hitting patients with anesthesia over and over again. And this patient was tiny." (According to the legal case against Gosnell, Mongar weighed ninety pounds.)

But even though Adrienne was no longer working with Gosnell, she always harbored the thought that some of what she'd done while employed there had been criminal and that she might one day be held accountable. Her name was undoubtedly on some of the paperwork, after all, and some of the women still working there knew and remembered her. Finally, that day came. But it didn't feel as she had suspected it might.

"The day that they came to my home and arrested me," Adrienne told me, "it was the most peace I'd felt in so many years. Because I finally felt like, *I don't have to hide anymore. I don't have to keep quiet about the things I've seen.*"

Adrienne pled guilty to third-degree murder and racketeering and spent twenty-eight months in prison.

YOU'LL RECALL that in chapter 6, I mentioned that my friend Kris and I prayed for and wrote to Kermit Gosnell and his arrested staffers. We'd done so for three years, never really expecting to get a response.

One day my phone rang. I don't remember what city I was in, but I was in a hotel room somewhere. It was August 2013. A female voice said, "Is this Miss Abby? My name is Adrienne Moton. I used to work at Kermit Gosnell's clinic."

My heart skipped a beat. Tears immediately came to my eyes. I smiled and thought, *Yes, I know exactly who you are. I've been praying for you every day for three years.*

We had a remarkable conversation. She was a bit guarded, of course, in that first call. We didn't talk much about her time in prison, but I knew she'd recently gotten out because I'd followed her story and the stories of the rest of the Gosnell group that we'd been praying for.

And why did she call me in particular? She said, "I just thought maybe you could understand where I was coming from."

I said, "Yeah, I think I do understand where you're coming from, at least in some ways. I've never been in prison. But I do understand what it's like to work in a clinic and to have to quit for conscience' sake." I didn't pepper her with questions. I wanted to leave room for her to set the agenda based on her reasons for calling and to share only what she wanted to. I wanted to hear her. I wanted her to know I was a safe person to talk to.

One thing she made crystal clear in that call was that she didn't want her face in the media anymore. I didn't get the sense that she was worried I'd call a press conference and talk about our phone call. She was saying, "I just want to live a normal life. Now that I'm out, I want to spend time with my daughter and my parents—I want to live a *private* life."

I think her daughter had been about fifteen at the time of her arrest. That was difficult for Adrienne. In fact, she told me being away from her daughter was the hardest part of being in prison.

I did ask her about her relationship with God. And interestingly, between the time she left the clinic and the time she was arrested, she'd had some "God encounters" that truly helped her find herself and her identity in Christ. And after she was arrested, being in prison gave her even more time to explore her growing faith. And that faith became increasingly important to her during those many months of thinking through where she'd gone wrong, where she should have put her foot down, where she should have drawn the line. She even said to me, "The best day of my life was the day they came and arrested me." Wow!

Interestingly, I learned that Adrienne never received my letters. She reached out to me because after she was released from prison, she started to tell her story to someone and they immediately stopped her. I think they didn't know what to say to the things she was sharing. They said to her, "You need to talk to Abby Johnson." She looked me up and called our hotline. It was truly a Holy Spirit appointment.

Coming out of prison in 2013 (she was released on probation because of time served in the three years awaiting trial), she was a completely different woman from the Adrienne Moton who had pled guilty and gone in. Completely redeemed. As always, redemption is a beautiful thing to behold, and I never grow tired of it.

When we finished that first phone call, I was so excited that I remember wanting to tell everybody—even strangers I passed in the hotel lobby—"Guess who I just talked to!" But I couldn't, of course, so I called Doug and said, "You know how Kris and I have been praying for and writing to those workers who went to prison because of the Gosnell case? Well, you won't believe it, but I just heard from one of them!"

"Well, that's awesome, babe!" he said. Which is pretty much Doug's standard response to anything I tell him. But then he added, "I know that means so much to you."

I would have loved to tell more people, but I had to stop with Doug because I wanted to respect Adrienne's privacy.

That call was the first of many between me and Adrienne. Even though she and I were restricted to phone conversations (she couldn't leave Pennsylvania because of her probation restrictions), we became friends. I loved her immediately. And she had plenty of questions for me too. She had never met anyone else who had worked in an abortion clinic but was now free of it and on the prolife side. Up until then, she had felt that she had no one to talk to—or at least no one who wasn't going to say, "Oh—you worked *there*."

In fact, during one of our phone conversations, Adrienne disclosed to me that on that day she first called me up out of the blue, she was timid and unsure how her call would be received—not simply because of what she feared she would hear but because of what she had *already* heard some of the prolife community say and write not just about Gosnell but about Adrienne herself. She did not expect to be well treated or welcomed by prolifers. At best, she thought she'd be labeled, and at worst, judged.

This should give us all pause. Kermit Gosnell's clinic was a national tragedy. But the door should always be open for any of us who've worked in an abortion clinic, no matter how horrific, to "step into the light," and once there, to live and work and worship in the light, not in the shadow of our past life.

We realize that our time in the abortion industry is part of our testimony—the darkness that God called us out of. But we want to be *well* out of it, doing and experiencing new things for the kingdom—activists for the cause of life, not just reminders of the evils of abortion.

So, here is my plea to you as you finish this chapter. When you minister to others—when you extend mercy—make every effort to see those to whom you minister through the lens of mercy. And not just mercy, but *fierce* mercy. Do you remember how we defined that word *fierce* in chapter 1? Marked by unrestrained zeal, intense, furiously active, and highly determined. Yes, be all that and more in seeing them as new creations. As equals before the Lord. Be alert to the temptation to see yourself as superior to those you serve. For if we see others as the forgiven sinners they are—*that we all are*—and accept them, then lives will be changed.

As you'll soon discover, Adrienne, in God's perfect timing, did eventually take some courageous steps to let her story be known, and so she has had a profound effect on audiences at some prolife events and beyond. Recently we were contacted by another woman who had been on Gosnell's staff, and I'm sure her approaching us had a lot to do with Adrienne's bold steps. My prayer is that the two of them won't be the last. Just think how sweet it would sound to hear more Gosnell staffers—and even Gosnell himself—speaking out for the lives of the unborn!

Mercy triumphs over judgment.

James 2:13

9

A DEEPER PURPOSE

The hotline at And Then There Were None rang, and I answered it. "Some boy gave me your flyer," a woman said. "I want to leave my job."

"Where do you work?" I asked.

"I'm a nurse in an abortion clinic in Louisiana."

Then she gave me the name of her clinic. I was well aware of its reputation for being a filthy, filthy place. *I bet you want to leave there*, I thought. "Where are you right now?"

"I'm at the clinic," she said. "I'm working."

"Do you need to call me back when you aren't there?"

"No. I don't care if they hear me."

"Okay. When do you want to leave?"

"Right now. I want to walk out right now." That didn't surprise me—I remembered feeling exactly the same way.

One thing I didn't know about Shelley when she called was that her son had just died. He was young, twenty years old, and had died unexpectedly without medical explanation. Even the autopsy had shed no light on the cause of his death. Later she told me, "One day I was sitting there, grieving the loss of my son, and I realized I was causing this same grief in other women."

Over the phone that day, I said, "Then grab your purse and leave. Call me when you're out."

She called a short time later and never went back.

Within days, Shelley called the hotline again. This time to tell us that one of her closest friends, another woman who worked at the same clinic, wanted to leave. This wasn't surprising; her clinic was owned by Leroy T. Brinkley, who had also owned Dr. Gosnell's clinic in Philadelphia. Shelley knew a lot about Dr. Gosnell and his practice. This, of course, made me think of Adrienne Moton, one of Gosnell's former staffers who'd served prison time. I couldn't wait to connect them if Adrienne agreed. I was thrilled when Adrienne welcomed the connection and the two of them developed a camaraderie based on their shared experiences.

It was the fall of 2013, and the quick-paced rhythm around the ATTWN office never seemed to wane. I loved that! I'm a high-energy person who loves making a difference in people's lives, and abortion workers like Shelley were making it abundantly clear that we were doing just that. However, Jennie and I, still the only two volunteers operating ATTWN, found ourselves running on fumes. We'd been at it alone for over a year, and even I had to admit we were stretched too thin. By this time, we'd assisted over sixty abortion workers in leaving the industry. At the rate we were going, it looked like by our second anniversary in the spring of 2014, we were going to double our first year's results, assisting about one hundred workers in only twelve months. We needed help! But our donations were modest, and we needed every penny for our "quitters." We had no funds to hire anyone, not even ourselves!

On the bright side, I'd come up with a model for how to move forward on a shoestring budget. We'd recruit client managers. These volunteers would serve as the primary point of contact for a worker when they came to us. They would befriend the client, help them with job leads, assist with their résumé, or make phone calls on their behalf. They would go through their budgets with them and see if ATTWN needed to financially assist them. The client manager is a client's go-to person.

And I knew just the person to pioneer this new role—Karen Herzog. Karen was working at Coalition for Life when I left Planned Parenthood, and she was the first one to befriend me when I became prolife. She had such a sweet, calming spirit about her. We were still very close friends, so I called to tell her my idea. Then I asked her, "Are you willing to take on a client or two at a time?" She said yes. And years later, she's still with us.

Karen got off to such a great start that soon I had more friends saying, "You know, Abby, if you ever need help, I'll take on a client or two." So, I signed them up. Before long, we had seven volunteers. I handled the training in addition to always serving as a client manager for a few clients.

There's no question, however, that figuring out how to best meet our clients' needs was trial and error, so we improvised. And boy we needed to! When I first developed the concept for ATTWN, the intent was that the organization would help meet the immediate practical needs of workers who were ready to quit but were being held back because they couldn't simply give up their livelihoods. Finding a new job or career after working in an abortion facility is tough. Many employers, especially in the medical field, don't want employees who used to work in the abortion industry. For a former abortion facility worker, crafting an enticing résumé that opens doors rather than slams them shut can be challenging. Also, the majority of people who have come to us from the abortion industry are single moms. They work long, hard hours. When they aren't working, they need to care for their kids, so when do they have time (or energy) to look for another job? They don't. They need a hand to hold, someone to help them, someone to come alongside them. And so that's some of what we can provide for them—while they're at work, we can be looking for jobs for them.

But I thought we would provide those practical needs, get them back on their feet, and then send them on their way. That's really all I had planned for. But these people needed so much more. Why hadn't I foreseen that? After all, my own emotional, spiritual, and relational needs were huge when I left my clinic. I should have known the same would be true of ATTWN's clients. Like Shelley, whose son had just died. Or abortion workers who had just experienced a miscarriage or stillbirth, causing them to lose their tolerance for helping mothers abort their babies. Or clients who were depressed, anxious, or spiritually searching. The complicated list of needs went on. Our client managers had to be able to field all these needs. It was important for them to be available at two o'clock in the morning when the worker had a nightmare and was freaking out or having a panic attack. They needed to provide emotional support to the best of their ability. And they did! I was so proud of our team and the difference they were making in these lives.

About this time, Pope Francis issued his first apostolic exhortation, titled *Evangelii Gaudium*, which means "joy of the gospel." I read it, and it struck me with incredible power. It also dovetailed with my growing realization of the scope of our clients' needs. This document was a life-changer for me. Nothing else had so clarified what my post–Planned Parenthood mission in life was to be and what ATTWN's purpose should be. How did it do this? For one, it emphasized the mission of believers to proclaim the gospel. And what exactly is the gospel? Pope Francis defines it like this: "Jesus Christ loves you; he gave his life to save you; and now he is living at your side every day to enlighten, strengthen and free you."[1] Cindy Wooden on the Catholic Herald UK website summarizes his writing this way: "Pope Francis says that the heart of the Christian moral message is love for one another, which must motivate Christians to share the Gospel, help the poor *and work for social justice*"[2] (emphasis added).

Since leaving Planned Parenthood, I had identified with the prolife movement because, if our goal as believers in Jesus Christ is to act on behalf of the poor and oppressed, then who is more oppressed, more powerless, more fatherless, and the least able to defend themselves than the not-yet-born? Isaiah 1:15–17 spoke volumes to me. It seemed to be written specifically for me!

> Your hands are full of blood!
> Wash and make yourselves clean.
>> Take your evil deeds out of my sight;
>> stop doing wrong.
> Learn to do right; seek justice.
>> Defend the oppressed.
> Take up the cause of the fatherless;
>> plead the case of the widow.

As I see it, if we're encouraged to "work for social justice," that includes not only discouraging ending the lives of the unborn but also discouraging the institution and system built up to profit from ending those lives.

Part of that process, from my perspective—and it's why I set up ATTWN in the first place—is to call abortion workers out of the industry that profits from ending the lives of the unborn and find other, more constructive places for them in society. That was more or less the extent of my original vision. A good vision, as far as it went. But now it didn't go far enough. And it was the pope's voice in *Evangelii Gaudium* that showed me what was lacking. His text clearly calls us to serve our constituency—in our case, disaffected abortion workers—in more than simply pragmatic ways: "An evangelizing community knows that the Lord has taken the initiative, he has loved us first, and therefore we can move forward, boldly take the initiative, go out to others, seek those who have fallen away, stand at the crossroads and welcome the outcast."[3]

Clearly, he was calling us to not only help satisfy the financial and practical needs of the workers who came to us but also to evangelize and disciple them.

So, that's what my mission needed to become! And to fully integrate that goal into our ATTWN mission, we would not consider our work on behalf of any individual ex–abortion worker fulfilled unless we had sought out that individual's spiritual needs and did our best to minister to them, either ourselves or by putting them in touch with others who might be better placed to meet those needs.

Let me tell you a few brief stories of some of those abortion workers.

Jayne

I got a call one day from Mike, one of the attorneys at Alliance Defending Freedom, who said, "I think it would be beneficial for you to talk with Jayne, a woman I'm working with. But I'll warn you—even though she has left Planned Parenthood, even though she's actively working to expose the atrocities at the clinic she worked at, she's still pro-choice."

It wasn't the first time I'd heard this. There are people who, exposed firsthand to the excesses and violations of the abortion industry, decide to act as whistleblowers against one particular clinic. They think, *Abortion itself is necessary, but this particular clinic* (in Jayne's case, one in Wilmington, Delaware) *is a bad clinic. Not all of them—just this one.*

Mike connected us, and before long, Jayne—who was still adamantly pro-choice—and I were on the phone with each other every few days. I would tell her, "I understand that you're pro-choice. I'd still really like to get to know you." I really loved her. She was such a firecracker. It had taken a lot of spunk and courage to walk out of Planned Parenthood and then expose all she knew. Every time we talked, I knew that at some point in the conversation she would say, "You know, I'm still pro-choice."

Eventually I said, "Jayne, you don't have to keep telling me that. I want to be your friend even though you're not prolife. I want to be your friend because we've both had to make very similar life-changing choices, and those choices were incredibly hard. And I want to be your friend because I just like you. I like your personality. You may be pro-choice for the rest of your life. That wouldn't affect our friendship."

And she did indeed stop telling me that she was pro-choice. Within a couple of weeks, I heard her using a different term entirely. "I'm not prolife *or* pro-choice," she said. "I'm just pro-health. I'm a nurse. I work for people's health."

It was, I believed, a significant change. She wasn't crossing the line all the way to prolife, but she also wasn't identifying

as pro-choice any longer. "I'm just here to give all the information," she said. "I'm pro-health."

Over the next several months, our relationship grew, and
I believed I was detecting changes in her outlook. And Jayne
being impetuous, all-in Jayne, when the change came, it came
with complete confidence and in no uncertain terms. "You
know what?" she said over the phone one day. "I'm prolife
now. I don't think abortion is okay at all. Ever."

Wow, I thought. "That's great, Jayne. Really. But this is
a new direction for you, and it's a major change. You don't
have to jump into anything right away. Take some time to
get your balance. Do some research. Make sure you're firm
in your conviction. And definitely don't make this change
because you think it's what I want to hear."

"Really, this isn't 'right away,'" she said. "My mind has
been slowly changing for months now. And you know what?
I've decided to work for the abortion pill reversal hotline."

This was a function that wouldn't have even existed just
a few years ago. Currently, women can take the RU-486
pill to induce a chemical abortion. And many people don't
realize there's a protocol that will reverse it—if a woman
changes her mind about the abortion and follows the protocol early enough after taking the RU-486 pill, she can
save the life of her baby. The hotline needed nurses, and
Jayne decided that was the perfect role for her. And in fact,
she's still doing it.

Mother and Daughter

Even though all that happened within less than a year after
my first contact with Jayne, it was still a change that slowly
revealed itself over a period of several months. Sometimes
that's how it happens with the workers who come to us.

Over and over at ATTWN, we are reminded how God works with each of us according to our needs. For instance, we had two abortion industry workers come to us—a mom and daughter pair. They approached us not because they had changed their mind and were now prolife but rather because they were unhappy about workplace rules at the Dallas Planned Parenthood clinic where they worked. They felt they weren't given enough breaks, and they weren't given enough time off for lunch to allow them to eat their meal in comfort. They had no particular convictions about abortion itself one way or the other, but they certainly got angry that Planned Parenthood wouldn't let them eat chips at their desks! "Is that against some labor law out there?" they asked.

Although the mom and daughter weren't prolife, as with Jayne, we built relationships with them, initiated conversation, and tried to facilitate healing. It didn't take long for those of us at ATTWN and the mom and daughter to realize something deeper was going on.

Here's what I mean. If I'm in Washington, DC, at the March for Life, I'm probably busy—and I may not have time for lunch. If a break comes along when I can grab a bite to eat, great—but if it doesn't, well, I didn't come to Washington to eat lunch. I came to march for the lives of tens of thousands, hundreds of thousands, millions of babies who can't act on their own behalf. I came because I was called to. I came to do something good. The fact that this pair was concerned about whether they got to eat chips at their desks was a good sign that they lacked a sense of mission for what they were doing.

We dug deeper with that mom and daughter, hoping to determine what that "something deeper" might be. After months of relationship building and in-depth conversations with their ATTWN client managers, we discovered, along with them, that they'd lost their heart for the abortion work they were doing. Both mother and daughter are now, like Jayne, 100 percent prolife.

Not everyone who feels the need to come to ATTWN will have the same perspective and the same beliefs when they come, and that's okay, because not everyone will have had the same experiences.

Nick and Adam

Nick and Adam (not their real names) were a couple—a gay couple—who worked in IT in the abortion industry. They came to ATTWN asking, "Will you help us—even though we're gay?"

And I said, "Of course."

ATTWN is a ministry. We want to speak life and truth into the lives of those who approach us. But to do that, when people first come to us, we need to find out what their physical needs are and commit ourselves to helping them with those first. We'll never be able to help them spiritually until they know that they're not on the verge of losing their home or starving to death.

With Nick and Adam, our first step was to help them find new jobs outside the abortion industry. And since they both worked in IT, they were very employable.

Then they told us they wanted to get involved in a church. With a heterosexual couple, we'd have first asked questions like, "What's your denominational background? What church have you been attending most recently? What do you hope to find in a church home?" But with a gay couple, there's a whole different set of concerns. We would want to make sure, for instance, that we weren't sending them to a church where they would be treated harshly and judgmentally—a church that would leave them feeling battered and browbeaten rather than loved and encouraged.

They were living in Georgia but were planning to move to New Jersey because one of them had family there. I talked to the pastor of a church in New Jersey near where Nick and Adam were headed, who said, "Well, we don't support gay marriage, but we would love to have them in our congregation. We have a program that I think would be great for them." So, we sent them to that church, and they made some good connections. They didn't remain a couple much longer—they had an amicable split. And that was a good thing, because they had decided their relationship wasn't very healthy. Both Nick and Adam had gone through serious sexual trauma as children, and that still-unhealed trauma was manifesting itself in their relationship.

Nick is still involved in that church and has decided for now that living a chaste life is the best choice for him. Adam, who no longer attends that church, is in another homosexual relationship. But whether they had remained a couple, continued living as gay men, left that church or stayed—we would have loved them anyway.

What if, when Nick and Adam first contacted us, we had said, "No, sorry, we don't help gays." Where would they be? Still in a highly dysfunctional relationship? Without a church home where they could not only be ministered to but also, at least in Nick's case, find a place to serve in ministry themselves? If we claim to be believers in Christ, if we love his heart and seek to emulate it ourselves, then we must learn to love anyone who comes across our path, no matter what lifestyle they're living, just as Jesus did with the woman at the well (John 4) and the woman taken in adultery (John

8:2–11). In the case of the woman caught in adultery, Jesus encouraged her to refrain from sin—but to both he offered his support and companionship *as they were right at that moment*, without first insisting they change to be more holy, more like him. When I come across people who engage in sinful or hateful behavior or conversation, my attitude is this: *If the Holy Spirit convicts and empowers them to change their lives, then that's between them and the Holy Spirit.* I can't be the one convicting them. For one thing, that's not my gift, and for another, if I tried to pressure someone to change their life to conform to my idea of what a sinless life should be, then even if their life changed at first, it probably wouldn't stick. Not without the Holy Spirit indwelling and supporting them in that change.

At ATTWN, we try to love people where they are; we try to show them where to find God's mercy and grace. We let God do the rest. After all, if the prolifers who prayed every day outside the Planned Parenthood clinic I managed had withheld their friendship and prayerful support from me because I was willfully involved in the abortion industry, where would I be?

Annie

Annie directed an abortion clinic in Chapel Hill, North Carolina. When she went out to her car to go to lunch one day, somebody—she still has no idea who—had taken little slips of paper printed with "abortionworker.com" (ATTWN's website) and attached them all over her car. Like small Post-it Notes flapping in the breeze. "It looked like my car had fringe!" she said. "But it wasn't funny at the time. I was so mad—mostly because before I could go anywhere, I had to take them all off."

Annie's boss had seen her car papered with all those little slips, and when Annie came back from lunch, she said, "What were those things on your car?"

"Beats me—a bunch of little slips of paper advertising abortionworker.com."

Her boss, looking a little uneasy, said, "I hope you threw them all away."

"Yeah . . . sure," Annie said, thinking, *It sounds as if she's worried. Why wouldn't she want me to go to that website?* So, when she got home, she checked out our website.

For the record, telling someone to litter an abortion worker's car isn't something ATTWN would ever do. Whoever did that to Annie's car was acting on their own volition. But for whatever reason, it worked for Annie, and she ended up leaving the industry. And not only did *she* leave, but seven other workers left the clinic with her!

Since Annie was the clinic director, and since some of the rest of the staff left with her, that clinic—which is still open—had to slow down their schedule significantly. Back when I was a clinic director, Planned Parenthood said it took about six months to fully train a staff member in one of their clinics, so replacing eight workers in that clinic, including the director, couldn't have been easy.

Annie and her coworkers accomplished not one but two things. Eight abortion workers freed themselves from the horror of being responsible, day after day, for ending the lives of innocent unborn babies. And the void they left meant that the clinic had to devote so much of its time to finding and training new staff that they were performing fewer abortions. In fact, for a time that particular clinic had to stop doing abortions altogether.

All of that from a bunch of notes surreptitiously placed on an abortion worker's car. One never knows what it will take—a flyer, a note, a word boldly spoken at the right time, a line of prolife activists praying faithfully outside the fence of an abortion clinic—to change the mind of an abortion worker and set their life on an entirely different path.

Look ahead five years and imagine the preschoolers happily playing with their friends because that abortion worker did what her heart had been telling her to do and stopped providing abortions.

Doctors

As you've seen in the stories I just related, nurses and other abortion workers often reach the point where they've had enough and simply walk out one day and never go back. But I've found it usually doesn't work that way with doctors. Doctors take a long time to get out. I've never had a doctor call me up and say, "I want to get out—right now. How do I do it?" There are reasons for that. For one, a lot more is on the line for them financially in terms of lost revenue if they quit. Also, they may be under contract with a physician's office, the clinic itself, or other group practices, and they would have to buy their way out of those contracts. Even if they badly want to get out, they may feel stuck.

I'm in conversation now, as I write this book, with three physicians who don't want to do abortions any longer but haven't yet figured out the way past numerous hurdles. They're making a lot of money where they're working, and they first want to figure out where their income is going to come from so they can continue to make their mortgage payments. Besides that, they're often well-known in their community as the abortion doctor, and that might make it difficult for them to attract a new clientele if they suddenly opened an office as, let's say, a general practitioner. One doctor I know who left the industry after being a full-time abortionist had to move to a different town, where he now works for a community health center.

One of the three doctors I'm talking to said, "I can't leave the abortion industry, because if I do, I think my wife, who's accustomed to the sort of lifestyle we can afford with what I'm making here, will leave me." Is that an excuse he's offering because *he* doesn't want to give up the income? Maybe. But I can tell you that many of my conversations with doctors who are thinking of turning away from performing abortions revolve around lost income and lifestyle changes. And before you criticize them for being ruled by greed rather than principle, remember that it's easier for someone else, who's not facing a potentially huge loss of income, to decide what should matter and what shouldn't.

Another doctor who, after talking with us, decided to leave the industry had to sell much of what he owned to raise $200,000 to buy his way out of the contract he had with his medical group. But he was determined. "Whatever it takes," he said, "however much it costs, we're going to do it." He and his family sold their home and their cars, and they lived in an apartment for a while.

Not surprisingly, that level of commitment is rare among the doctors I talk to. What I'm more likely to hear from them is, "I don't want to do abortions anymore, but giving up everything? That's too much to sacrifice." And I remind myself not to be too critical of them. None of us want to be impoverished or uncomfortable. We feel that we've worked hard to earn the lifestyle we enjoy. It's scary to think about something threatening it or taking it away, much less giving it up voluntarily. We Johnsons don't have a huge house, but we have one big enough to house all of us comfortably. I can't imagine taking my family to live in a three-bedroom apartment. With all our kids? It would be incredibly difficult.

Still, many abortion doctors tell me, "I did not become a doctor to do abortions all day, every day. That's not why I spent all that money and all those years and all that hard work in med school."

How did the doctors who have called us up at ATTWN hear about us in the first place? Most of the time, it's from someone else, such as a sidewalk advocate, who talked to the doctor and steered them my way. That first conversation leads to another, and another. But it usually takes months for them to finally say, "Okay, I've made up my mind. I want to stop performing abortions."

One of the three doctors I'm talking to now worked at a clinic that received one of our mailers. It was passed around the clinic—not to provide information to its employees, of course, but rather to mock us. When the doctor saw it, he was curious. *This organization says it helps abortion workers. Does that include doctors? If I decide to leave the industry, would they help me?*

I'm still fascinated by how effective these mailers are. Many of them are seen by a person, like that doctor, who's dissatisfied with their job for some reason and secretly thinking, *Would they help me?* Many of the workers who come to ATTWN say, "I just folded up that flyer, put it in my scrubs pocket, and took it home with me. Later, I realized it was speaking directly to me." One doctor who left the industry was walking into his clinic one day when a sidewalk advocate gave him a copy of my book *Unplanned*. He read it—and then emailed me.

That's the mystery and wonder of it. When we send those mailers, God knows what point of crisis a worker will be at when they read it. Only God knows which ones will slip it into their pocket because they're frustrated or lost. Some of the workers who have walked away from their clinics are caught in serious substance abuse problems, often brought on by their work. Annie says that every day when she worked at Planned Parenthood, she would go home and drink a bottle of wine. After she left her job, she was able to get sober.

As you can imagine, once we at ATTWN had a taste of this kind of real, gritty, hands-on, life-changing ministry, we wanted to be able to do even more. So, I started seeking God's counsel. "Lord, what else could we do?"

And that gave birth to the idea of holding healing retreats. I'm eager for you to read about them, but as you do, I want to encourage you to consider *your* deeper purpose. Obviously, something (should we agree Someone?) motivated you to pick up this book, and you've read this far. Perhaps Micah 6:8, the closing verse of chapter 1, has taken on new meaning for you:

> He has shown you, O mortal, what is good.
> And what does the Lord require of you?
> To act justly and to love mercy
>   and to walk humbly with your God.

If so, be eager to explore with God how he might deepen and expand your mission. It's been my experience, as you will see, that the deeper we grow with God, the deeper we'll go for God.

But you are a chosen people, a royal priesthood, a holy nation, God's special possession, that you may declare the praises of him who called you out of darkness into his wonderful light. Once you were not a people, but now you are the people of God; once you had not received mercy, but now you have received mercy.

1 Peter 2:9–10

10

HEALING THE DEEPEST WOUNDS

'm sorry to be critical, Abby, but I don't get it," said a fellow prolifer at an event we were both attending in 2014. "By focusing on getting abortion workers new jobs outside of the industry, all you're really doing is creating a revolving door of workers. How is that really helping in the cause for life?"

Believe it or not, I actually appreciated the question. It was honest, open, and direct. And I could tell she wasn't so much criticizing as she was trying to understand.

"It's not only about getting them out," I said. "It's about guiding them to a relationship with Christ. I'm not just concerned about getting them a new job. I'm concerned about their salvation. And their healing. We have over a hundred people who now have life in Christ. Isn't that something to celebrate? And the ones who do take their places? Well, we'll be there for them too."

But many people in the prolife world just weren't getting it. I think it's because they weren't seeing the transformation in the lives of our quitters. We were. They weren't. And the reason was that before 2014, we didn't have any quitters who were willing to come forward or who we felt were ready to be put in the public eye. They were still healing. They needed privacy and time. And many, once they were ready, needed help and coaching on public speaking and media. That took money, which was still tight. But most of all, it took time.

Time. If anyone understands that healing takes time, I do. I walked out of my clinic in October 2009. But the scene from my life that you are about to read took place in early 2015, nearly five and a half years later.

AT FIRST, I couldn't bring myself to pull into that parking lot. I drove by at least three times before I finally turned the wheel.

The building I kept driving past had, at one time, been the Planned Parenthood clinic where I had served as director. I no longer lived in College Station, Texas, but I'd had an appointment there that day, and afterward I decided to drive past my former clinic to see the changes I'd heard had been made to the building. Or at least that's what I told myself. I immediately noticed the absence of the heavy fencing out front and the bars on the windows that once served to keep out prolifers.

Most people who drove by would see just a building. If you knew the story behind the building, and if you were prolife, you might see it as a victory. But when I looked at the building, I saw sin. So many sins. And many of them mine.

I looked at that building and saw eight years spent without God. Eight years of time lost. Eight years of lost opportunity. There was, however, a part of me that saw the building as a triumph, and that's what finally enabled me to pull into the parking lot. Instinctively, I parked in the second-to-last spot, the same spot I had parked in for eight years. But as I was about to turn off the car, I decided I was unwilling to follow my old playbook in any way and moved my car closer to the building.

Once I parked, I sat for a moment inside the car, scanning the building's windows for some sign of what might be going on inside and checking whether anyone was there. Light shone through one of the windows—the window to my old office. The light shining, I knew, was situated right outside one of our old education offices; it was never turned off.

Well—it wouldn't hurt to go look, just from the outside.

I walked up to my office window. It took my breath away to see my old desk still sitting there. But I could see more than a desk. I could see, in painful memory, myself sitting at that desk, auditing charts, checking to make sure the ultrasound pictures of the babies we killed were in every chart.

Thousands of those ultrasound pictures flashed through my brain, the pictures of the perfectly round heads of those innocent babies. We measured the heads to find out how far along the women were in their pregnancies. On the shelves of my office, I could imagine the folders containing the lab records of each woman who'd had an abortion. I could imagine the folders containing the products of conception examination sheets, the papers we signed when we had found all the body parts after each abortion.

I could see where the bowl of miraculous medals had sat on my shelf—medals left in our flower beds by the prolifers who prayed at our fences. (For you non-Catholics, miraculous medals are worn around the neck on a chain. The Virgin Mary appears on one side.) For eight years, I picked up all those medals and kept them in that bowl.

Something was missing—the small conference table that had sat next to my desk. That was where I interviewed applicants, lying to them about our "mission" at Planned Parenthood. "We want to reduce the number of abortions," I would tell them. But we didn't care about reducing the number of abortions any more than we cared about the women who came to us. We needed abortions because that's how we earned money. The time I spent with job applicants at that small table was my first opportunity to mislead potential employees about all of the "good" we were doing.

I looked through the next window to the right: a small room with a kitchenette. Anyone would recognize this as a staff break room, but what I saw was our staff standing around the table, grabbing a bite between abortion procedures. I saw us laughing as the abortionist told us his greatest "abortion stories." And as he did, we would look out this very window and mock the prolifers lined up outside along the fence, praying for all of us.

I continued around the building and looked into each window. I had been in every one of those rooms. I could see myself there, convincing women to have abortions, reassuring them that they would feel no regret afterward.

From one window, I couldn't see into the recovery room; I could see only the doorway. But I could recall what I'd seen in that room every day for eight years: women sitting in large leather recliners, many of them crying as they realized what they had done. The recovery room is the saddest place inside an abortion facility. Every woman cries. We gave them twenty minutes to dry their tears and convince themselves that what they had done was normal. They had to convince themselves that the emptiness they were feeling was simply hormones.

I could see myself cleaning the blood off the floor in the exam room where one of my friends began hemorrhaging after the abortionist perforated her uterus. All that blood. As my friend lay on that exam table, white as a ghost, I begged the doctor to allow me to call an ambulance. "No ambulance," the doctor replied.

I could see all of it. Memories I hadn't thought about in over five years were suddenly rushing in, and I couldn't control them. I was sobbing and clinging to the stone wall for support as I reached one more window.

Through that window, I could see across a hallway into the products of conception lab, where I had stood sorting and counting the body parts. So many babies. So many tiny faces. So much horror. My legs couldn't support my weight anymore, so I just sat on the ground and wept. I was in full view of the street, and people driving by could see me, but I didn't have the will to move. It felt as if my heart were breaking—and not just figuratively. It was physically painful.

I have no idea how long I'd been sitting there with my face in my hands when I felt a hand on my shoulder. I looked up, startled, to find a stranger, an older man, standing there. *He must think I'm crazy*, I thought. But in my pain and confusion, the only explanation I could offer him was, "I used to work here."

He looked at me with such compassion. In a gentle voice, he said, "I know. I know who you are. Can I help you?" I tried to stand up, but I was so wobbly, he took my arm to steady me. We walked across the parking lot. "Do you want me to call someone?" he asked as I got into my car.

I didn't. I couldn't think of anyone who would understand what was happening inside me at that moment. "No thank you. But you've been so kind. I'll be all right—really." I watched him walk away, and then I couldn't resist going back to the window of my old office one last time. There was a Bible verse written on the wall, no doubt placed there by the 40 Days for Life folks who now owned the building. It said something about evil. That was not the verse I had envisioned writing on that wall one day. Since leaving Planned Parenthood, I had wanted to come back and write 2 Corinthians 5:17: "Therefore, if anyone is in Christ, he is a new creation. The old has passed away; behold, the new has come" (ESV).

I walked back to my car and pulled out of the parking lot. I knew the numbness I felt would eventually go away. I turned on my iPod and hit shuffle. It was no coincidence, I'm sure, that the song that started playing was Matt Maher's "Alive Again."

I drove home thanking God to be alive again, to be alive in him. My past cannot be changed. Those memories, those pictures that flooded my mind as I peered through the windows of my old clinic, will always be a part of me. And I don't mind—those memories keep me motivated in this battle. I know I am forgiven. I know God has cast my sin as far as the east is from the west. I feel his redemption. I feel his mercy. I feel those gifts every day of my life.

Sometimes when I share experiences such as this one, it feels awkward—and definitely not easy or comfortable. I guess through this book I'm still healing in public, as I discussed in chapter 3. But awkward healing is better than no healing at all. It is worth the pain and embarrassment if it helps others comprehend the toll that abortion takes on one's soul. Until one truly understands that toll, they won't understand the importance of fighting abortion, whether by praying for its end, getting involved in the legislative process, ministering to women in crisis pregnancies, reaching out to women who've had abortions or abortion workers, or whatever other ways God may lead.

I'm excited to now take you inside of one of the most powerful healing experiences that God has led us to offer at ATTWN—our healing retreats. As I'll explain, each time I lead one, God takes me deeper into his healing mercy. And although at these retreats my healing isn't fully in the public eye, it still takes place in front of several other women, women who are struggling with many of the same issues I've struggled with since leaving Planned Parenthood. All the women at these retreats were active in the abortion industry, and then, like me, they left. But they couldn't easily leave behind the feelings of guilt and grief because of what they'd done.

We have three different kinds of retreats. First, we have Phase 1, or healing retreats, which are small—a maximum of eight women plus a staff of three. Our healing retreats are open to anybody who has come through our ministry. Our Phase 2 retreat is simply a continuation of Phase 1 but digs deeper into what was shared in Phase 1. Then we have a larger annual retreat at which we have thirty or more quitters in attendance. My goal is to see all or most of the women who attend Phase 1 and 2 retreats follow up by attending one of our annual retreats, where they can meet others who have gone through the program. Some really awesome lifelong relationships have been developed at these annual meetings.

Our first healing retreat was held in January 2015. My intention during the planning of the retreat had been to serve as a facilitator, which I did, but I got as much out of it as the rest of the attendees. The camaraderie of being in a group with other people who had sinned and suffered in the same ways I had, and who were gradually healing in the same ways, was something I had never experienced before. Our group sessions, as well as our conversations during the unstructured time, were filled with comments such as the following:

"You felt that way? Me too!"

"Oh yeah—I dream about that too."

"Really, you too? I thought I was the only one."

At that first retreat there were also many thrills and surprises for me. One was that my good friend Annette was able to attend. (You first read about her in chapter 2. She was the one who called my name backstage and was the first Planned Parenthood worker I helped to leave her job.) Another was that my son Carter (my fourth child, born August 2014) was baptized that same weekend—and Annette came to both events! Annette and I had developed a wonderful friendship. And that is the goal of ATTWN—to not only identify the workers who want to leave the abortion industry and help them do it but also to build warm relationships and genuine friendships with them. The retreat helps foster those friendships.

We've honed and improved our format and our content since the first retreat. Now, we start on Friday night with what might feel like a typical group therapy getting-to-know-each-other session: "Hi! Where are you from? Why did you choose to come this weekend?" And then it gets a little closer to the bone: "Why did you get involved in the abortion industry in the first place? What were your primary responsibilities at the clinic? Why did you choose to get out?" These sessions can be intense, but in reality, that's the easiest part. The retreat gets tougher as the weekend goes on. But as straightforward as that first night is, and despite the fact that attendees are surrounded by women who have had similar experiences, it still gets very emotional for them. Having to admit the role they played in the deaths of so many babies . . .

Saturday is an intense all-day round of therapy. We start with something called the APS—the Arno Profile System. It's a test developed by the In His Image Institute of Counseling and Training based on a set of fifty-four questions and takes only a few minutes to complete. We print out the results and give a copy to each participant. It tells us which of the four basic temperaments they have: melancholy, phlegmatic, choleric, sanguine. Your temperament doesn't necessarily drive behavior. But knowing your God-given temperament is important because it can help you prevent behavior that you might be innately drawn to. Many of our participants, when they understand this and find out their temperament, grasp for the first time why they've always tended to behave in certain ways even though they knew it wasn't good for them. What an eye-opener that is!

Very lively discussions always erupt after this. After all, the women there have all experienced, and been guilty of, similar things. We don't force any of the women to share anything they don't feel comfortable volunteering. We simply let them share whatever they *want* to share. And, of course, they *all* end up sharing, despite the fact that they've usually just met each other for the first time that weekend.

The first time I ever took the APS, I laughed the whole way through it. I thought, *There's never been a more right-on test of my personality! For better or worse! This is me!* The report we give them describes what each of the four personalities tends to do, think, and feel.

Those Saturday morning group discussions are amazing. We start by talking about what parts of our temperament led us to work in the abortion industry. We talk about the difference between shame and guilt. For me, guilt is feeling bad about *something you've done.* Shame is feeling bad about *who you are* because of what you've done. Big difference. We all feel guilt at times simply because we're all guilty. Romans 3:23 says, "For all have sinned and fall short of the glory of God." Do I feel guilty about what I did during my years in the abortion industry? Yes, and I should—I did terrible things. But I don't feel bad about who I am. God has made me into a new creation. I'm not the same person I was then, so for me to feel shame about the old me would be to negate what Christ did on my behalf. If anyone in one of our discussion groups is struggling with a load of shame or guilt, we can help them.

Participants also set some goals for the weekend. Things they would like to work on. It is a healing retreat, after all, and they can't know how to heal if they don't know what they're healing from. And by that point in the retreat, the discussions and the input they've received from the APS have revealed to them quite a number of things they need to be healed of. For instance, when I first walked away from Planned Parenthood, I sat down and estimated the number of abortions that I had likely been a part of. I felt a need to somehow quantify the depth of my accountability—of my guilt. As painful as that was, I found it to be helpful in my healing, so we do the same thing in our retreats. We have our participants calculate the number of abortions they were accountable for. How many abortions per week did the clinic perform? How many days did they work? Were they guilty of all of them or just some? Did they have an actual hands-on role? We have them work out a number, just as I did. And that process is very emotional for them, as it was for me years ago. Some of our participants have estimated that they were accountable for over a hundred thousand abortions.

"Okay, now that you have this number," we say, "let's figure out how to heal from it." As Christians, we talk a lot about God's forgiveness. Talking about it is easy, though. *Believing* that God forgives us? After we've done something horrible? That's harder. But we can usually manage it after a while because we realize that God is God—and he's filled with love and tender care for us. So yes, in the end, we can believe that God has forgiven even us. It's forgiving *ourselves* that's hard. And part of the way we at ATTWN try to facilitate that difficult task is by talking about what we have done, and talking about it publicly. Getting it out. Not holding it in. For many of the women, the retreat is the first time they've spoken to anyone about their participation in abortion. Shame lives in our secrets and in our silence. The things we don't want to say. So, in our retreats, we break that sound barrier and talk about all these things—no matter how painful, no matter how poorly they reflect on us—and we do it out loud. The participants feel very raw by the end of this session. And exhausted. We take a break.

The next step is to have them write their admission of guilt. And we don't restrict this to their time in an abortion clinic. They can list anything they want to heal from. It could be infidelity in their marriage. The poor relationship they had with their kids—or parents. The cutthroat attitude they've had about their ambitions, whatever the cost in collateral damage. A bad temper. Hatred. Racism. Any troubling issues that have caused them to struggle.

Once they have those statements written out, we break into a couple of small groups and acknowledge to each other what we need to heal from. This acknowledgment begins the process of casting aside our guilt and shame over these things.

On Saturday evening we talk about the cycle of dehumanization. Anytime there is human tragedy, it's human nature for people to look for someone to blame. We feel a need to find the culprit. I believe that when abortion was legalized in the 1970s, at first the blame fell on the women having abortions. But when the pregnancy center movement got underway in the mid-1980s and into the 1990s, the dynamic changed. People said, "We can't shame these women. They are victims too—victims of our society's systemic approval of abortion. In order to save these babies, we have to help these mothers. If we shame them, they won't come to us."

But if we can't blame the women who are seeking abortions, who can we blame? Well, the workers. Isn't that the natural progression? The blame must lie with the workers administering the abortions. And to blame them, first we have to dehumanize them—by calling them "monsters" or "the devil" and saying terrible things about them. Sadly, as we have discussed before, there has been a tendency within the prolife movement to first dehumanize and then accuse the abortion clinic worker.

Enter ATTWN. One of our goals is to *rehumanize* these workers, which leads to also rehumanizing the children lost to abortion. These babies are not just numbers, and not just a category. They're little individual human beings who would have grown up to have personalities and families and lives that made a difference. And that leads to rehumanizing the prolife movement itself, helping prolifers understand that our battle is not against individuals. We should not be blaming individuals here. The problem is systemic—and it's caused by the sin of a broken world. If we see it as a fight between me and another person, an us-versus-them problem, toe-to-toe and nose-to-nose, then we've missed the point.

ATTWN has been moderately successful in this area the past several years. And that's reflected at our healing retreats, since the women who attend have themselves been dehumanized by the prolife people standing out on the sidewalk. Our attendees have experienced further dehumanization on Facebook and other social media. Our goal at the retreats is to bring humanity back to all of them—the women and also the babies lost. We can't rehumanize all twenty thousand or so babies that any one woman at the retreat helped to kill; that would be overwhelming. So, each former worker chooses a specific abortion scenario that for one reason or another stands out in their mind: one abortion, one mother who came to the clinic and left without a baby in her womb. We ask each participant to remember that mother, that baby, and to rehumanize that child.

They are offered opportunities to do that in different ways, but one specific task we ask each woman to do is write a letter to that baby. They may name the child or not. That's up to them. They choose the details, but we do say, "You're going to write a letter to this baby. And then when you go home, do something to memorialize them."

They can decide for themselves how to memorialize the baby to whom they've written, but we provide an excellent suggestion. ATTWN has a partnership with the National Memorial for the Unborn (https://www.memorialfortheunborn.org), outside of Chattanooga, Tennessee. Inside their building are little brass nameplates mounted all over the walls—probably tens of thousands of them. Each plaque bears a baby's name or perhaps some little sentiment. People have purchased these brass nameplates in memory of a baby aborted or otherwise lost. Sometimes a nameplate is purchased and personalized by the woman who lost the baby, sometimes by the father or grandparents, sometimes by the person who paid for or assisted with the abortion and later regretted it. Three of the plaques on their walls are ones I purchased: one for each of my abortions and one for the baby I saw being aborted. The National Memorial for the Unborn is a place people can go to grieve and find healing. If you place a plaque on the wall, they will send you a replica of your nameplate mounted on marble. Beneath it is written: "Displayed at the National Memorial for the Unborn."

Outside they have a peaceful sanctuary called Remembrance Garden, with engraved brick pavers that memorialize babies lost to miscarriage. For any child who is memorialized at the museum, they will send a marble plaque to hang in your home. This is a beautiful way for our workers to memorialize a child, whether it was their own or the baby they are remembering as part of our retreat.

Before the retreat ends on Sunday, we offer the women the opportunity to read aloud the letter they wrote to the one baby they chose. Then we give them counseling tips and goals based on their temperament. Each of the four temperaments has its own patterns, characteristics, strengths, and vulnerabilities for which we give them some guidelines and reminders for setting better boundaries before we all break and head for home.

Where did the content for our retreats come from? Did we hire a therapist or psychologist with experience in emotional healing to design a program for us? No—as we approached the first retreat, I looked at what had worked for me, since my experience was similar to that of the women who would be coming. What had given me the strength to overcome my grief, guilt, and shame because of what I'd done? What had helped me find a new, more constructive path in life? I had done all those things that we now do with the women at the retreat, and I had found them very helpful. I had written a letter to the baby. I had gotten a plaque for him. I had calculated my "abortion number." And it had brought me healing. I had also tried a lot of things that made me feel terrible—some of them useful even so, such as writing an admission of guilt. But unless I had been willing to be vulnerable, to be humbled before God and before my friends and acquaintances and even before people I'd never met, right out in public, I would not have experienced the process that now helps women at our retreats find healing for their deepest hurts. I have already seen how these women, who have likewise humbled themselves and become vulnerable, are now able to become agents of change and healing in the lives of many others.

The activities at our retreat have a healing effect, but they're painful to go through. In the end, many of these women—their hearts cleansed—decide that their place in the world now is making what contribution they can toward ending as many abortions as possible.

At every retreat, I stand amazed at how God's mercy penetrates the pain of each participant, including mine. After our first retreat, I realized that until I started ATTWN, I'd been walking my healing journey alone with God. I thought I'd started ATTWN to help other clinic workers. What I hadn't realized was how much I needed it for myself. Now that I'd experienced the community of healing together with others at the retreat, I knew even more clearly that God had led me to begin ATTWN.

Women arrive at our retreats spiritually, emotionally, and relationally bound by the chains of abortion. They are haunted by memories. Weighed down with guilt. Held captive by shame. But God's mercy—his tender compassion and his healing touch—shatters the power of those chains. I watch in awe as wounded and hardened hearts are healed and downcast spirits are set free.

This makes me think of a dramatic story in Mark 5. Jesus arrives in a lakeside town by boat. No sooner does he climb out of the boat than a man comes running up and falls on his knees in front of him. This man lived among the tombs. Day and night he would cry out and cut himself with stones. He was possessed by demons. People of the town would often chain his hands and put irons on his feet, but he'd tear the chains apart and break the irons. No one was strong enough to subdue him, and they couldn't bind him anymore so he roamed free, in agony.

What follows is a fascinating dialogue between Jesus and these spirits, whose name is Legion. Jesus commands the spirits to come out of the man, and they ask to be cast into a herd of pigs. Jesus agrees, and the next thing you know, this herd of two thousand pigs stampedes down the bank, into the lake, and drowns. It must have been quite a sight. The men who'd been herding the pigs go running through the town reporting what happened and soon a crowd gathers around Jesus. And there they see this tortured man sitting calmly. The demons are gone. He's in his right mind.

The townspeople are so spooked by this that they beg Jesus to leave immediately.

There is a touching scene in verses 18–20. Jesus is getting into a boat to leave and the man is begging to go with him, but Jesus won't let him. Instead, he directs the healed man to go home to his own people and tell them how much the Lord has done for him. So the man does. I love the closing words of verse 20: "And all the people were amazed."

I know exactly how they felt!

Jesus . . . said, "Go home to your own people and tell them how much the Lord has done for you, and how he has had mercy on you."

Mark 5:19

11

JUDE'S GIFT

Imagine my husband, Doug, a stay-at-home dad, at home with our kids—four of them at that point. It's 10:00 at night on a chilly February evening in 2015, and, of course, the kids are all in bed. The youngest, Carter, nearly seven months old, is lying asleep in the crib next to our bed. Where am I? On the road, as I often am, at a speaking engagement.

Before turning out the lights, Doug scrolls through Facebook for a few minutes. He checks my page to see if I've posted any news, and there he finds a brand-new post:

> If you adopt through an attorney privately, and not through an agency, do you have to have a home study?[1]

To some husbands, that might have seemed like a mildly puzzling question. But Doug was used to my impetuousness. Even through the internet, he could no doubt hear the wheels grinding in my head, and even more so, in my heart.

I was up to something. But what? And was it too late? Was it already a done deal?

Adoption wasn't a new concept for our family. We had discussed it often, and both Doug and I considered it part of the Official Johnson Family Plan—our *distant future* plan. Preferably far enough in the future that our youngest wouldn't be just seven months old.

So, forty-five minutes after my original post, Doug posted this response:

> What is going on here? Why do we need a home study all the sudden?[2]

And a few minutes later, one of my Facebook correspondents posted that she was on the edge of her seat waiting to hear where this was going.

Clearly, our adoption plans had become high internet drama—and we didn't even have any adoption plans!

As life often does, this had come at us out of the blue.

A few minutes later, my cell rang, and I didn't have any trouble guessing who was calling. I was laughing when I answered.

Doug had a million questions.

"Are you crazy?"

"Whose baby is this?"

"How did this even come up?"

"Did I mention that we have a seven-month-old?"

"What does your mom think?"

"This isn't the plan!"

I filled Doug in. My best friend, Kris, knew a woman in crisis who needed a family to adopt her baby—a baby who was due in just a month. The birth mother (to protect her privacy, let's call her Beth) knew about me and our family through Kris. She was very comfortable with the idea of us adopting her baby.

Fine, but how did *Doug* feel about this idea that he'd had no inkling of just a few minutes before? "Why doesn't Beth have this all figured out by now?" he asked over the phone that night. "She's known for months she was having a baby."

"She had a plan, but it fell through," I said. I went on to explain.

Beth was married and had three kids. But she was separated from her husband, and during their separation, she'd begun seeing another man. He'd treated her well at first. And she hadn't been treated well by a man before—certainly not by her husband. Unfortunately, it didn't take Beth long to realize that her new boyfriend drank heavily. Things turned violent. He assaulted her several times—and then he started in on one of her kids.

Beth moved out and found a safe place, but she soon discovered she was pregnant. Many women would have aborted that inconvenient child—but Beth never even considered it. Still, the question remained: What to do with this child? Neither her estranged husband nor the baby's biological father would be any help—in fact, she wanted as much distance as possible between both of the men and herself and her kids.

Doug knew me well enough to know that, even this quickly, I was completely committed to this unborn baby and 100 percent ready to say yes, just like a child bringing home a stray pup and asking, "Can we keep him?" I'm sure he could hear it in my voice. But it had to be a joint decision, obviously, and I could hear things in Doug's voice too. He was bewildered and far from ready to commit to this child. He would need time.

At first, time didn't help. He woke up the next morning convinced that there was no way we could adopt this baby. Bad timing. For now, he felt, it would be too hard. When our kids were older, when I wasn't traveling so much, an adoption would definitely figure into our plans. But right now? No.

My phone chimed with a text from Doug saying he was strongly inclined to say no.

Once I was home from my trip and Doug and I had a chance to discuss it, we agreed on a plan: we would see if any other families stepped up first. Indeed, Kris had told us a couple other families were interested but not yet committed.

Neither of those families worked out.

For me, there was no question what I wanted to do. I loved this baby already, and I was all in. But Doug still had his own decision to make. After all, he would be doing most of the care for the child. He made his list of questions.

"If I say yes, do we have enough energy in the tank to get through another year with a newborn?"

"Will I be able to bond with the new kid?"

"If I say no, will Abby or anyone else see me as less of a man or father?"

"What if an opportunity like this doesn't happen for us again?"

Doug and I discussed his concerns and objections. We spent time in prayer; we went to our parents for advice. And we both knew there was a ticking clock—this baby was *on its way*! We started some of the adoption paperwork just in case. We had our home study and lined up attorneys both for us and for Beth. The ball was rolling.

It took Doug only a few days to decide—and his answer was yes!

And I loved his reasons. I'll let him explain:

Every time I looked five, ten, thirty years down the road, I couldn't see my life without this child. In my heart and in my head, I had already made him part of our family. In my mind's eye, I saw him playing in the yard with our other boys. I could imagine his high school graduation and fixing his tie before his wedding. There were visions of my dad teaching him to shoot a gun and ride a horse. At this point, there was no way I could say no. How could I remove him from my heart when he already had such a firm grip on it? For Abby, it was instant, but for me it took some time. I needed to be reminded of how awesome our little family is. That our children love each other, and we all take care of each other. Like Abby says, we are open to all life. That includes the lives that God injects into our lives out of the clear blue sky. Sometimes you have to forget the script, allow yourself to be uncomfortable, and ride the wave.[3]

LIKE THE OPPORTUNITY to adopt Beth's baby, our family situation had just kind of snuck up on us. Or maybe it would be more accurate to say that my old patterns of being addicted to work at the expense of my attention to our family were still an area of ongoing struggle for me. Our decision back in 2011 for Doug to become a stay-at-home dad was perfect for us but had allowed me to slip back into my unhealthy balance between work and family life. We'd then become pregnant with Alex that October, and once he was born in July 2012, we had only two months before I was pregnant again. And then babies kept coming. With four children and my intense schedule, we'd never reached a point where it made sense for Doug to go back to work. My work for the unborn was a priority for both of us. Besides, Doug continued to love being a stay-at-home dad. It fit him. It fit us. Nevertheless, we had an unsolved problem. And the fly in the ointment wasn't Doug. It was me. Here I was, ready to adopt a new child when I wasn't fulfilling my full role co-parenting the children God had already given us. My urge to do more and more in the fight for saving the unborn never went away, even as our kids arrived one after the other.

"Why can't you just be with us?" Doug would ask.

And my answer would be, "Because this is important."

And he would respond, arms spread wide to take in our very young children, "*This* is important. Right here." My drive, my commitment, came at a cost. And unfortunately, my family paid most of that cost. Even when I was home, much of the time I wasn't actually present with them. I would be looking at my phone or checking my email—constantly distracted.

The kids might say, "Mom, look at this."

"Okay," I would say, but I wasn't really looking.

Or at bedtime they would say, "Mom, lie down with us." And I would lie down beside them, but I would be on my phone the whole time, paying no attention to that rare and precious moment that would never come again. At the dinner table, they would all be talking about their day, and Doug would be interacting and keeping the conversation going, and I would be responding to an email. Dance recitals, camp performances—I may have been there physically for so many of these once-in-a-lifetime moments, but even so, the experience was lost on me.

It wasn't that I wasn't bonded with my children—I definitely was. I felt like their mom. I didn't feel as if there was distance between us. And yet, if Doug and I were both in the house and the kids had a need, which one of us did they cry for? They always went to Doug. He was the one who could make things better for them, and they'd learned that through experience. Mom was often not at home, and when she was, she was distracted. That they went to Doug didn't really trouble me. I would even say to them, "You need something? Go to Dad. Dad will help you."

I felt a real closeness with my children. When I would come home from a trip or even a long day away from home, they would rush to greet me and grab hold like limpets, like Velcro. They wanted me. They wanted my attention. Too often, though, as soon as I'd taken off my coat and kicked off my shoes, I had my phone out and was right back at it— so, too often my kids didn't get the attention they craved.

Although I could be distracted by the needs of the women with whom I communicated, I truly loved my kids. I loved being around them. I just hadn't figured out how to mother them.

If you had asked me for the "plan" behind my approach to work-life balance during that period, it would have been frighteningly simple. I would have said something like, "Okay, I'll have the babies. That's my role and something only a woman can do. Then I'm going to go back to work at my job that, again, I'm uniquely qualified for. And Doug is happily at home, keeping things running there, which he does so well. Our kids are safe. So now I can go work at saving other people's kids. I'll be a mom when I'm home, but my everyday role is to work."

It's not that I didn't have a good motherhood role model. My mom was a stay-at-home mom, and a great one. Always attentive. I was just obsessed with working. I felt as if I only had value when I was working. That's so appalling and also so common that I'm going to repeat it: *I felt I only had value when I was working.*

Now, considering the adoption forced me to once more do some "dangerous" praying—praying for God to reveal my root problems, have mercy on me, and help me to heal. And in no time flat, I saw something I'd missed when I first tried to address this issue back in 2011. Or perhaps I should say, something I hadn't been spiritually mature enough to understand back then.

As the requests for speaking engagements and media appearances continued to come my way, in my broken way of thinking, I often felt as if I *couldn't* just go do something with my family without first responding to an urgent email or taking a phone call. Why? And this is important: The reason I worked such long hours wasn't because I didn't want to spend that time with my kids and my husband. I *wanted* to be with my family. I just felt as if I didn't have a choice—as if people were depending on me (and I was depending on myself) to go out there and speak eighty times a year, and do all the interviews, and be on all the TV shows, and show up at the Texas State Capitol five days after my baby was born to fight for legislation. In my mind, my job was more important than *indulging* my desire to be with my children! After all, I'd been the director of a Planned Parenthood center that performed abortions. I'd had two myself. If anyone had the responsibility to end abortion, I did—if only to make up for all the pain I'd caused, all the abortions performed, the tiny lives lost at my clinic. I was saving lives and saving souls. When I was working, I felt a sense of reparation: the more I worked, the more babies I saved, which helped to make up for what I had done for eight years at Planned Parenthood. Right?

Of course, once I understood and admitted that reasoning to myself, I recognized what was broken in my thinking. I was seeing *myself*—my efforts, my words, my presence—as personally responsible and capable of ending abortion!

"Abby Johnson," I had to admit, "just who do you think you are? God?" Ending abortion wasn't an Abby-sized task. It was a God-sized task. And my efforts would *never* measure up to the size of that task. Not only that, but I couldn't "pay the penalty" for my sins against women and the unborn through all the efforts in the world. Nor did I need to! For Jesus had paid that penalty already through his death on the cross. My debt was paid. The burden lifted. The mercy already poured out on me. All I had to do was accept that mercy. And *I* wasn't saving souls or saving lives. God was!

My part was to play the roles God had given me and play them to the best of my ability. And prolife activist wasn't my only role. God had blessed me with four children (so far!) and therefore had called me to the vocation of motherhood.

The opportunity to adopt brought about this wrestling with God. And this wrestling with God and subsequent realization opened up a whole new river of mercy in my life—a river from God, to me, then through me to other women. I so relate to many of the other moms I talk to who are having a hard time figuring out the balance of motherhood. How do we balance, on the one hand, the sacred trust of being a mom with, on the other hand, performing well in our careers? Many women struggle to find that balance.

Don't get me wrong. I'm not saying I have accomplished that balance. But I understand the need for it in a way I've never understood until God gave us the gift of adoption. And I understand *why* that balance is worth seeking and striving for and evaluating on an ongoing basis. In fact, God never stops growing us and revealing deeper levels of his mercy to us. Our part is to take the risks God presents to us and be open to his deep work in our spirit.

So, when Kris first contacted me about a baby being available for adoption, that was the state of affairs in the Johnson home. We had four wonderful kids, a stay-at-home dad doing all he could for them and for his work-obsessed wife, and a mom who too often couldn't disengage from work long enough to watch her kids perform in the Sunday school Christmas program but who now had the wisdom to understand *why* she must break that pattern.

And then came Jude.

But the wisdom that comes from heaven is first of all pure; then peace-loving, considerate, submissive, full of mercy and good fruit, impartial and sincere.

James 3:17

12

THE BOND

Adoption is beautiful—but also very emotional. It's the most beautifully heartbreaking thing I've ever gone through.

I love that Scripture speaks of God adopting us as his children. I don't believe I ever fully understood what it meant that God had adopted us until Doug and I adopted Jude. Take a look at Ephesians 1:4–8:

> For he chose us in him before the creation of the world to be holy and blameless in his sight. In love he predestined us for adoption to sonship through Jesus Christ, in accordance with his pleasure and will—to the praise of his glorious grace, which he has freely given us in the One he loves. In him we have redemption through his blood, the forgiveness of sins, in accordance with the riches of God's grace that he lavished on us.

These verses tell me that God chose us "before the creation of the world" (v. 4), just like Doug and I chose Jude before he was even born. He did it "in love" (v. 4) and "in accordance with his pleasure and will" (v. 5), just as Doug and I fell in love with Jude and adopted him by choice and with heartfelt pleasure. What we give to Jude as our son is given "freely" (v. 6), just as God gives us eternal life freely. And maybe the part that makes my heart smile the most is "in accordance with the riches of God's grace that he lavished on us" (vv. 7–8). Oh yes, we "lavish" on Jude all that we have, just as we do with our birth children.

Is it any wonder, then, that adoption forms a bond between parent and child that lasts a lifetime? Understanding the bond I feel with Jude, my chosen son, helps me understand the bond God feels for me as his chosen, adopted daughter. And that understanding increases the bond I feel with God, my Father. A bond that grew richer through the experiences you are about to read.

JUDE'S DELIVERY CAME much sooner than we had expected. Because of the birth mother's worsening preeclampsia (a life-threatening situation for both mother and baby), his birth date was moved up to March 12, a mere *two and a half weeks* after we'd first heard about the opportunity to adopt him. I wasn't able to be present for Jude's birth, much to my frustration, because I was speaking on the West Coast. Nor was Doug because he was home with the kids in Texas. But our friend Kris, who was also a close friend of the birth mother, Beth, was there—not just in the hospital but in the delivery room, coaching Beth along and texting Doug and me with updates on Beth's progress: "Pushing . . . she's pushing . . . still pushing . . . HE'S HERE!" Then Kris cut the cord. Jude was the only one of our kids for whom Doug did not cut the cord. But we couldn't have had a better stand-in than Kris. One of Kris's friends, Jessica, is a photographer, so many of the texts we received during and just after the birth were accompanied by photographs, such as the severing of the cord.

The next day, I was at the small hospital where Jude had been born. It was March, and cold still, so I was wearing a sweatshirt—an ATTWN shirt, in fact. I was so nervous that day! Kris was already there waiting with Beth, and I texted her as soon as I got to the hospital. She and Jessica came down to the lobby and took pictures of me walking to Beth's room. Beth was sitting in the chair beside the bed. Although this was the first time I'd met Beth, I knelt by her chair and embraced her. We must have hugged for at least five minutes.

All the time we hugged, I was crying, Beth was crying, Kris was crying, Jessica the photographer was crying . . . Everybody was crying except Jude.

Beth, I had already been told, was deaf. There wasn't concern that Jude would be deaf because Beth's deafness wasn't hereditary. It was a birth defect caused by a medication her mom had taken when she was pregnant with Beth.

Beth asked me if I wanted to hold him. Of course, I was dying to—but I'd wanted Beth to somehow give me permission. I didn't want to just come in, scream, "Here's my baby!" and snatch him up. Because, really, he was still her baby then. But when she asked me if I wanted to hold him, I picked him up eagerly, still crying, and studied every detail of his little face and hands. Out of the corner of my eye, I saw Kris and Beth holding hands and watching me. Beth's head rested against Kris as she continued to cry. There were lots of tears that day, especially for Beth, who suffered such a conflict of emotions. She was about to relinquish to another woman the raising of the baby she'd just given birth to, and that reality was undoubtedly just setting in for her. The difficult circumstances of the baby's conception were also still on her mind, I'm sure.

I wanted to be careful not to force her into anything she was uncomfortable with. I'm sure I asked her about a million times throughout the process, "Are you sure about this? Doug and I will help you however we can, whatever you decide—whatever you need."

And again and again, Beth said, "No, this is what's best for him. This is what has to happen."

Grace, eight years old at that point and eager to meet her new baby brother, and Doug arrived the next day. Just like Beth and I had immediately clicked, she and Doug really clicked as well. Beth is still very much a part of our family life, and she tells Doug all the time, "I'm so glad you're Jude's dad." And Jude really has turned out to be a daddy's kid. He thinks I'm all right—but he *really loves* Doug. Isn't it funny how God gives people what they need? If Beth had chosen to keep Jude, he wouldn't have had that close, loving relationship with a male parent during his young years.

The hospital let Doug, Grace, and me stay the night in a hospital room. They asked us, "Do you want to keep the baby with you?"

But Doug and I turned to first ask Beth, "Do you want to keep him here in your room?" She said yes. And we were fine with that. Frankly, we'd have been okay with her breastfeeding him those first days. But she had already made the choice not to do so. But she did pump milk so as not to deprive the baby of the nutritious colostrum only the birth mother can provide.

The next day Beth went home—Kris drove her—and Doug, Grace, Jude, and I went to Kris's house. (When I'd flown up to meet Jude, I'd brought a little baby car seat with me—I was prepared to bring him back!) We all left the hospital at the same time to share together every minute we could. The attorneys had already been to the hospital so that Beth could sign over temporary guardianship to us. She would have thirty days to change her mind, but I was confident she wouldn't.

Over the next two days, before Doug and Grace needed to go home for Grace to get back to school, Beth came to Kris's house to spend time with us and the baby. Grace was so pleased to have one more baby in the family! After Doug and Grace went home to Texas, I stayed with Kris another twelve days, and each one of those days, Beth came to be with us. During those many hours we were together, I got to know her and she got to know me. That may sound strange to many, but we had always planned on an open adoption—we wanted Jude to know his birth mother.

On day thirteen of Jude's life, we were at Kris's waiting for a telephone call from the Texas Interstate Compact for the Placement of Child office (ICPC), which had to approve my return to Texas with Jude. Just the day before, I had asked Beth one more time: Are you sure about this decision? Do you want to change your mind? And her answer was the same: I am sure.

My mom had flown from Texas to accompany us home, so she got to meet Beth too. When we hadn't yet heard from the ICPC, I decided to stay at a hotel by the airport so I'd be ready to hop on a plane as soon as they called. Mom had come with me to the hotel, but the next morning, unsure when we'd hear back from the ICPC, she decided to head back to Texas and meet us when we got there. Finally, at noon the call came—Jude and I had been okayed to come home. I hung up, giddy with joy. *Yes! I'm going home today!*

I immediately went online to buy a ticket and found a flight on Southwest. Only one problem—it was flying out of an airport almost two hours east. But that was fine! I didn't care. I was going home.

I got there in time for my 3:00 p.m. flight, banging through the airport carrying not just Jude but all the baby stuff—car seat, diaper bag, etc. I was one of those women you always see in airports that make you say, "Boy, she's gutsy—flying by herself with a tiny newborn and enough gear to outfit an expedition to Everest."

The Southwest ticket clerk said, "How old is your baby?"

"Fourteen days old today," I said proudly.

And he said, "Well, you'll need a doctor's note saying it's okay for him to travel. It's required for any babies fourteen days and under."

And I thought, *Why couldn't he be fifteen days old?*

Frantic, with one eye on the clock because the "plenty of time" I had started with had now become "I'm going to miss my flight if I don't hurry," I called our pediatrician's office back in Texas and explained the situation. "Can you fax a note to the airline?" I asked.

And our pediatrician said, "Uh, no. I've never seen this child."

Oh. Yeah.

Fortunately, while we'd been waiting to come home to Texas, I'd taken Jude to a local doctor for a checkup. I desperately called that doctor, and they said they would fax a note immediately. But as I stood at the counter, eyes on the fax machine, I began to wonder whether they knew the meaning of the word *immediately*. Then it was there, and Jude and I, my heart racing, rushed through security and onto the Jetway just in time for our flight.

I settled into my seat, calming myself with thoughts of our joyful arrival in Texas and the excitement of bringing home a new baby. The official adoption would take place in Texas. I couldn't wait.

JUDE'S PRESENCE in our home forced me to make a conscious decision. *Now we have two infants, just seven months apart*, I thought. *I can't leave Doug with all this responsibility. It would be too much—all his time would be going to the babies, and the older kids would feel abandoned. Besides, I've been spending my time on work and giving it my concentration—and not focusing on my family. I've decided to change, in major ways. I have to create boundaries to protect my kids and my time with them. I have to learn to be truly present.*

And there was a second factor as well. Doug and I had agreed to take this woman's child and raise him as our own. That was a sobering responsibility. It was no greater than the responsibility we bore for our own children, of course, but it was a powerful reminder of the obligations and privileges of parenthood. The new bond I felt with Jude intensified my bond with my birth children. For all their sakes, I had to change. I *wanted* to change. Right away!

That decision made a major difference.

I began not only to watch from a distance as my children lived life but also to live life with them, participating fully. I started being more intentional about being fully present when I was home. I evaluated my travel so that I could be home more often, even if it meant turning down important trips. And that was especially true during the fall and spring, which were typically heavy travel periods for me. My motto became, "Whether or not the work I am doing on the road gets done by the time I reach my front door, it stops there. When I'm home, I'm home with my husband and kids, and they have my attention."

And I won't kid you—that was hard. I had to turn off my phone some days because I was constantly feeling an urge to look at it. Jude was born in March, and by summer I realized that, to stick to my resolution, I would have to set a strict schedule. No more working until nine or ten at night! I would decide each day what my work hours would be, depending on need (for example, "Tomorrow I'll work from ten to three"), and then hold myself to it.

This new arrangement meant more than just setting up some new rules and boundaries, though; it required me to frequently review my personal mission that I discussed in the previous chapter. I had to remind myself that it isn't solely my responsibility to end abortion. That is a God-sized task.

Yes, I desperately want to be part of making that change in our culture. But I can't and am not expected to do it on my own. I must remind myself that I'm one of a great number of people doing what I can to end abortion. Of course, I'll do my very best. But I do so by playing my part in reflecting God's mercy, in finding and keeping that balance between work and family that so many working mothers strive to find. I must be able to say, "I'm always going to be behind on work stuff. I have to learn to be okay with it, because I can't change that. I'm never going to reach the end of the day with my inbox empty. There will always be a list of things to do first thing tomorrow morning that I had hoped to get done today. Sometimes people will have to be okay to wait."

The way that plays out in real life for me is to tell myself, "Okay, my inbox is full. So what? It's time to get the kids into their pajamas, brush their teeth, and tuck them in. Or I have twenty-five unread text messages, but my kids want to go to the water park and it's a beautiful day, so we're going. Now." I have to internalize the truth that my children are more important than anything on my work calendar or in my inbox or voice mail. I have to remember that my vocation is not to be a public speaker. My vocation is to be a wife and a mother. With that as my foundation, I also minister to others as a prolife advocate and activist.

Too many people in Christian ministry have failed their own families at home because they were spending their lives trying to save other people's families. I had to keep in mind that such a failure is the height of hypocrisy. A hypocrisy of which I'd been guilty. But God's mercy covers that. For guilt can lead to repentance, which leads to forgiveness, which leads to peace.

JUDE BECOMING part of our family introduced a whole different dynamic. It meant that Beth was a presence in our family as well—and not just a philosophical one. She spent time with us. Many adoptive families make a different choice. For reasons of their own, they prefer a closed adoption and their adoptive child never sees or talks to their birth parents. Because our adoption of Jude was wide-open, when Jude became a part of our family, so did Beth.

We wanted Jude to truly know his birth mother and for Beth to be able to experience all his childhood milestones. And that decision had both joyful and painful consequences. For instance, for the first year, even in the midst of my joy over having Jude and loving him and watching him achieve all the first-year accomplishments—first steps, first words, etc.—I also felt a distinct, undeniable sadness for Beth. A sense of loss. I often felt that I couldn't rejoice because somewhere Beth was sitting, unable to experience these same things as his mother.

Oh, we communicated almost daily, Beth and I—through texts, of course, because Beth is deaf. And I sent her photos or videos almost every day. I filled her in on everything. And she shared some things with us in person, as she usually sees Jude about once a year. But I felt that as the one who had the privilege of seeing Jude through all these things in person, I was the wrong person to comfort his birth mother. I had benefited from her loss. Fortunately, Kris helped Beth because she lived near her and really could be there. And she was faithful to remind me, "Now would probably be a good time to send Beth a card from Jude."

Some adoptive parents might have a hard time understanding our decision. But for me, our adoption situation is almost like co-parenting. Is he legally ours? Yes. Does he live with us? Yes. But when major issues come up, we tell Beth. We ask for her opinion. We even wanted to name him something that she loved and approved of.

Beth's other children are involved as well. And they're so sweet—one boy and two girls. The girls write little cards to Jude—to "our little brother." It's neat.

A whole lot of people love this kid, and I want him to grow up knowing all of them.

OUR ATTORNEY HAD TOLD US, "December 2 will be the day you'll show up in court to finalize the adoption. Don't be late. And generally, the judge wants to see the whole family, so bring all the kids."

Great, I thought. *Yeah, fantastic—let's bring a bunch of wild toddlers into the courthouse.* But we wanted to make a good impression on the judge, so that's what we did—with the help of our friend Heather and my mom, who came along to help us manage our little troop. We took the time and thought to dress them all especially cute. Jude, too, of course. We had him dressed in adorable little overalls. But— and any of you who have kids will identify with this—he had a huge blowout in his diaper. I mean, it was everywhere. And this happened not at home where we could have quickly changed him into another outfit but in the courthouse while we were waiting for our name to be called.

Now, like any other family with babies, we always have extra clothes in the diaper bag. Always. But not that day. And it was almost time for us to be called up. As we stood in the hallway, we took stock. There were cutesy little shops around the courthouse, but none of them opened for another hour.

"We can't take him in there naked," I said. "Or in just a diaper. How would that look?"

Doug nodded, thought for a minute, and said, "Well, I guess I'm going to Walmart."

As he drove away, I thought, *Walmart isn't all that close. The judge is going to call us before Doug gets back.* No sooner had that thought gone through my head than we got the call. "I'm not going in there with a baby with no clothes!" I told our attorney. "The judge will take one look and say no."

"I'll tell him we need a few more minutes," she said.

Finally, after what felt like forever, the door burst open and Doug rushed over to me. He handed me a Walmart bag and started to say something, but I ignored him, ripped open the bag, and pulled out . . . a camouflage shirt and pants. The front of the shirt said, in big neon orange letters, *H-U-N-K*.

I'm sure my eyes were the size of tennis balls when I looked up at Doug and held up the outfit as if to say, "What in the world is this?"

"I swear," Doug said, hands open and up in self-defense. "It's the only thing I could find in the right size."

So, there we were, the rest of our children with hair nicely done, looking cute in their Sunday-best outfits—and Jude as HUNK. In camo.

Mom was helpful. "Try to wrap a blanket around it when you're holding him," she said.

The judge was ready for us. As our group filed into the courtroom, we saw quite a crowd of people there to resolve their own issues. It felt to me as though they all looked at us and smiled, as if they were thinking, *Oh, look how cute.* Then it was our attorney's turn before the judge. They have a little dance they do, as if it were scripted—the judge asks something and the attorney responds, and you get the impression they've both read from this script innumerable times before. Then the judge asked us, "Is it your desire to adopt this child and make him a permanent part of your family?"

"Yes."

He said, "And what will you name this child?" Because at that time his legal name was still Beth's last name.

We said, "Jude Christian Johnson."

And he said, "That's a great name," and signed the papers.

Everybody in the courtroom applauded. It was a great moment. Really sweet.

And so, the HUNK joined the family.

Mercy, peace and love be yours in abundance.

Jude 1:2

13

OUT OF THE SALTSHAKER

can take absolutely no credit for the name of this chapter. It is from the title of a book written by Rebecca Manley Pippert and first published back in 1979. Its full title is *Out of the Saltshaker and into the World*, and it's about effectively sharing your faith and making evangelism a lifestyle. My compliments to Rebecca for coming up with such a very clever title and writing a bestselling book still so alive and relevant to us today that it was reissued yet again in January 2021.

The book's title, which I'm borrowing because it fits this chapter so well, is based on these words of Jesus:

You are the salt of the earth.

Jesus made that declaration during his famous Sermon on the Mount in Matthew 5:13. We all know that since ancient times, salt has been used to flavor and preserve food. But salt had many uses, including being a good antiseptic, and served other important purposes to the people in Jesus's audience. He used it for his illustration to appeal to his listeners to live up to their purpose. He went on to say,

> But if the salt loses its saltiness, how can it be made salty again? It is no longer good for anything, except to be thrown out and trampled underfoot.
> You are the light of the world. A town built on a hill cannot be hidden. Neither do people light a lamp and put it under a bowl. Instead they put it on its stand, and it gives light to everyone in the house. In the same way, let your light shine before others, that they may see your good deeds and glorify your Father in heaven. (Matt. 5:13–16)

Be salt in this world, be light, Jesus is saying, so that others see not only the difference you are making but also God at work through you and give him the glory for the result.

I resonate with the idea of getting out of the saltshaker, which sits on a shelf in storage just *waiting* to be used, and getting busy *doing* what we were made to do. As you've seen, I don't sit still very well at all. Discovering and doing what I was made to do is the journey I've been on since leaving Planned Parenthood in 2009. You've been tracking some of that journey through this book. You've witnessed the birth and growth of my understanding of God's mercy and the practical ways God has helped me experience and live out his mercy, both in motherhood and as a prolife activist. You've followed the birth and early years of And Then There Were None, so you've seen the "salt" at work—the ministry reaching out to abortion workers with practical help, emotional help, and most important of all, spiritual help as we disciple and evangelize. ATTWN and I are both out of the saltshaker.

In 2016, someone extremely special to me was ready to come out of the saltshaker as well. Adrienne. After the former Gosnell staffer called me in 2013, she and I developed a rich friendship. But in truth, I'd already been connected to her for three years before that while I prayed daily for her after the Gosnell story first broke. I watched in awe as she grew in the Lord and began her deep healing from her years of witnessing and participating in the atrocities of late-term abortions. Here, in Adrienne's own words, is just a sampling of the memories she had to heal from.

I walked briskly into the procedure room one day to begin prepping for an ultrasound, and as I did, I came face-to-face with a twenty-nine-week-old baby (at least that's what was written down; he looked more like thirty-six weeks), who was all alone. The baby had miscarried from the womb of a seventeen-year-old girl after we induced her with Cytotec. My two coworkers had left the baby boy there in a dish for which he was too big. His large hands, feet, and shoulders were extending out over the edges of the dish. He made me gasp. I looked at his serene little face; he seemed to be asleep. His large, fully formed body caused me to feel something I hadn't before—sorrow. I took a picture, laid a cloth over him, and prayed for him. I knew what was going to happen to him next, just as soon as Dr. Gosnell entered the room. A gallon jug in the freezer awaited him, and the doctor never put complete, whole babies in jugs.

Horrified and suddenly with new eyes that could see what was being done—and what I was a part of—I ran out of there. I was trying to get away, but that was ridiculous. The baby in the dish simply wouldn't leave me.

(You can read more of Adrienne's story, and the stories of our other quitters, on our website, https://abortionworker .com/quitter-stories/.)

In 2016, after completing her probation, Adrienne accepted my invitation to attend that year's healing retreat. I was beyond thrilled. Adrienne was nervous about coming because she was a former Gosnell worker, and she knew everybody at the retreat would know of the horrors she'd taken part in. Even among abortion workers, Gosnell's actions had been unthinkable, so she expected condemnation. Imagine her relief when what she experienced was a group of women who understood what she'd been through and what she had to live with now, and who loved and accepted her from the moment she arrived at the retreat.

One of the other former abortion workers at the retreat, Julie, had been out of the abortion industry since the mid-80s but had never told anybody that she had worked at an abortion clinic. Her friends didn't know. Even her children didn't know. No one knew—other than those of us who knew her through And Then There Were None.

Julie is a sweet lady inside but has a very tough exterior. At one point during the retreat, Adrienne was talking and became so moved by what she was admitting to us that she began to weep. Julie stood, came to the front, and stood behind Adrienne's chair. She put her hands on Adrienne's shoulders and said, "Here's how I see it, Adrienne. You were the sacrificial lamb. All of us here have worked in the abortion industry. We've done the things that you've done. But you're the only one here who was held accountable by our justice system. It should have been all of us. It could have been any of us. You are our sacrificial lamb."

That was a beautiful moment for all of us, but especially for Adrienne because it reinforced for her that all of us at ATTWN see her as being just like the rest of us. As an equal. And we see ourselves as just as culpable as she was. Again, here are Adrienne's own words:

> And Then There Were None took me in and loved me, with Abby making it clear that she didn't see much difference between their lives and mine, according to Scripture. *All* sin is redeemable by the work of Jesus on the cross, she said. It was the most powerful thing I had ever heard.

Yes. *All* sin is redeemable by the work of Jesus on the cross. That is the truth of the gospel. That is the power of God's fierce mercy. It is the most powerful message any of us can give others. And it is the work of us, the salt of the earth, to spread that message.

Adrienne experienced so much healing at the retreat that she has since become very involved in our recurring healing retreats. There she ministers to others. She is out of the saltshaker!

ONE OF THE MOST BEAUTIFUL results I've witnessed at our retreats is when former abortion workers discover that, because of the healing God has brought into their lives, they now have the privilege and the power to bring healing into one another's lives. As in Julie's case above. She arrived at the retreat feeling broken and empty and unlovable because of her past. But when she found herself standing up and moving to the front of the room to take a place behind Adrienne, she discovered that she had the power to speak healing words into the life of another worker. This realization has a tremendous effect on women who, until that discovery, see themselves as takers of life, not healers. I watch as this transformation takes place at every retreat. Eyes light up. Faces soften. Tension eases away into relief. And God's healing touch multiplies from one life to many. That is the mystery and the reward of being God's salt in the lives of others.

Our retreats have not only been a source of healing for new quitters. I've also continued to heal at every retreat. I've found them to be a source of community like no other. In today's world, it is so easy to live in isolation. But I don't believe that's how we're meant to live. I believe we were meant to live in community with one another. Healing springs from community, for it is there that we discover we are not alone in our sin or our sorrows.

I recall a time I felt painfully alone. It was early in my prolife days, and I was in a meaningful conversation with a prolife leader I respected. I was being open and vulnerable, which is my normal inclination. (With me, it's WYSIWYG—what you see is what you get.) In that spirit, I confessed that when I was at Planned Parenthood, my colleagues and I used to call the freezer that we put the babies in "the nursery." This friend had never been an abortion worker. He looked at me, shock on his face, and said, "You can't ever share that publicly. The prolife movement can't handle it."

I was deeply embarrassed. Of course he was shocked. How could I have done that, right? It was awful that we said such things. How callous and disrespectful. What a mockery we were making of the precious lives we were taking.

I realized that his intentions were good—he was trying to protect me. He knew I needed to find a place in the prolife world, and he was afraid a statement like that would invite judgment and condemnation. But even so, in that moment, I thought, *So, among prolifers I can't talk about what I've done and been a part of? Is there no place for me? I don't belong in the pro-choice movement anymore. Is it true that I can't really be me in the prolife movement either? Do I need to hide behind some facade to make everybody else feel comfortable?* That encounter was really a blow. I felt so completely isolated.

It wasn't until I was in our retreat setting, with other women who'd said the same kinds of things and understood where I came from, that I thought, *I've found my people. These are people I can be me in front of. I can speak out. I can say whatever I need to say in order to heal and nobody's going to look at me and gasp or judge me or say, "How could you do that?"*

This sense of community at our retreats allowed all of us to heal as we expressed the thoughts, feelings, and actions that needed to be addressed. One refrain I've heard at every retreat is this: "I saw the same women coming back for abortions over and over again. I thought I would be helping women by providing a medical procedure that would assist them with an unusual problem that would otherwise be negatively life-changing. What I felt was happening instead, when I saw those 'repeat customers,' is that I was simply enabling a careless lifestyle—enabling irresponsibility. I wasn't helping those women, at least not in the way I'd envisioned."

The subtext there, and it's what I think female abortion workers discover about themselves, is that although they might have believed at first (as I did) that their motive for working in an abortion clinic was to help women, after a while a disdain for women sets in. Before I left Planned Parenthood, I remember thinking, *Are they stupid? Does someone need to explain to these women how babies are made—and that there are ways to prevent it? Why can't they get their lives together?* I've heard it over and over again at our healing retreats: "Yes, it happened to me. I came to think that women are stupid, and that's how I treated them. Our male doctors treated them that way as well."

Of course, it's not a healthy situation to be angry with the women you're supposedly trying to protect and help. I discovered that I could help the former abortion workers by asking, "Why was it bothersome to you for a woman to have five abortions if you thought it was okay for her to have one? You weren't frustrated by the one, yet you were frustrated by five. In reality, your conscience was telling you that abortion is wrong—the first one was just as wrong as the fifth."

Within the community setting, it is helpful for the women to discover they are not the only ones who felt this conflict and they can help one another restore their appreciation for women as a whole and no longer disdain their own gender for being "stupid."

ONE OF THE WAYS ATTWN grew in its ability to be salt in the lives of abortion workers was that, financially, we were able to increase our staff. We'd hired our first paid staff member back in 2014—a vice president of administration and finance (essentially a CFO). I went out on a limb with that big title, praying we would eventually have the finances and staff to justify such a thing. Until then, our team, all of us in volunteer roles, consisted of only Jennie, our part-time doer of all things; Karen, a part-time client manager; and me. This decision was huge, as it allowed us not only to centralize all our dealings with money, donors, facilities, processes, and more, but it also freed Jennie, Karen, and me to spend more time ministering to our clients.

Then in 2016, we hired another client manager who also worked as a bereavement doula. She has experienced seven stillbirths and/or miscarriages herself and is uniquely gifted at walking alongside clients who've had either. We'd become aware of the need because we'd observed that abortion workers who suffered the death of a child through stillbirth or miscarriage were often struck by the horrible realization that in their abortion work, they were involved in bringing about the deaths of other women's children.

We also hired an intake manager, Kris. She answers the calls that come in on our twenty-four-hour hotline. Before we hired her, Jennie and I answered all our calls. She records the caller's information and ascertains their needs, processes their paperwork, gathers the required documentation, verifies that they work (or worked) at an abortion facility and whether they're still working there, and more. Then she gives the worker to an available client manager.

It's been amazing watching God at work when it comes to pairing a worker with a client manager. It's always a perfect fit. And we know that's not our doing. The Holy Spirit is putting these people together. We have one client manager who is a recovering alcoholic and drug addict. She's been sober for seventeen years. Every time we have a worker who is struggling with substance abuse issues, they're always partnered with Pam. The intake manager is totally unaware of that issue in the worker's life. She just gets their paperwork together. She might put a message out on our Facebook group saying, "Hey, I have a worker ready from Roanoke, Virginia. So, who's available?" And so far, if there's someone with substance abuse issues, Pam has been their client manager. I love watching God at work!

Speaking of God at work, he also surprised us in 2016 with the unexpected gift of a man who offered to come aboard as a résumé writer. He approached us with the idea. He owns a business as a professional résumé writer, heard about ATTWN, and wanted to volunteer his time. He works with every client to write their résumé and has been a game changer for us. Before he came on board, each client manager did their best to help clients with their résumé, but most of them probably would have said it wasn't their strongest skill.

Sometimes our clients don't have a résumé at all, so he'll create one from scratch. He is proficient at helping clients identify their abilities, including skills they may have picked up working in the abortion industry. After all, people acquire skills in all work environments, right? So not everything abortion workers take away from their clinic jobs is bad. He's even received a résumé that someone wrote on a napkin. He can turn whatever he's given into an amazing résumé.

He then preps the workers for their job interviews and goes over various interview techniques. Knowing that most interviewers will ask, "Why did you leave your last job?" he coaches them to be honest and direct and to say, "Well, I had a big change of heart on the issue of abortion." He role-plays other interview questions with them. And he writes cover letters for their résumés as well. He's done a great job of being honest but also getting their résumés to the top of the pile. Which is why many of the HR people who have hired some of our workers have said, "Your résumé was so beautiful, it was sitting at the top of our pile." It has been a huge blessing having him on the team.

We find it easy to work with the abortion workers who come to ATTWN because we can see firsthand how disillusioned they are about the clinics they work at, what those clinics are actually doing, and how desperate they are to get out. And that means they need and want to move on to the next job.

How hard is it to find them that job? It can be difficult if they are not licensed or certified. If they are licensed, however, it's not hard. If, say, they are a nurse or a certified medical assistant, it's easier to get them into their next position than it is somebody who had no previous medical experience before their abortion clinic job or for somebody who had no college education or official nurse's training. If all they had was on-the-job training, that's not enough for most prospective employers, so it's far more challenging to find them their next job. But challenge or not, we at ATTWN work hard to find our clients new jobs that will contribute to our world and be satisfying.

FINALLY, IN AUGUST 2016, I undertook the biggest "out of the saltshaker" initiative of the year. I launched the first-ever Pro-Life Women's Conference. I believe I was partially influenced to do so by seeing the continued stunning results of our healing retreats. It is a powerful thing to watch women step out of isolation and come together in community, sprinkling themselves as salt in the lives of the women around them, encouraging and cheering one another on in their growth, development, and healing.

I was also inspired by a spontaneous discussion at our annual ATTWN staff retreat when we all found ourselves sharing our dismay that so often in the political and religious arenas, male rather than female voices dominate the conversation about abortion. It's not that we disdain or resent men speaking about the issue, because abortion affects the entire human race, male and female. But abortion uniquely impacts women. After all, women are targeted for abortion. Our bodies are on the tables, and our health is at risk. The violence of abortion is happening against *women*. So rather than stand back and abdicate our leadership role in speaking into this issue, we decided to intentionally step up as leaders and make our voices heard. What better way to facilitate that than to hold a conference of female leaders in all aspects of the prolife movement? *Just imagine*, I thought, *what a "community" of women could accomplish together*. So, I said, "You know what? We just need to do this. We need to do a conference for women, by women."

I brought together some of my good friends, prolife women leader friends, and we began having conference calls once a month. We started talking about what the conference could look like and developed a plan. I made the decision that the Pro-Life Women's Conference must be more about what we are *for* rather than about what we are against. So, that's what we've done. We've made an intentional decision to include a ton of adoption advocates, resources, and groups that help women who have been given a diagnosis that their baby may have an abnormal condition. We also include information about prolife health care.

We decided that Dallas would be a convenient location because a lot of prolife organizations are located there and many of the women who were going to be presenting were not far from the Dallas area. So, in June 2016, we got it booked and had our first conference. We had keynote speakers, panels, and breakout sessions for the approximately five hundred women in attendance. And it seemed everybody loved the conference.

I didn't plan the event assuming we were going to do it every year. I just thought, *We'll do it once and see how it goes.* From the podium, I told the audience, "I don't know if we're going to do this every year. Maybe every other year or once every five years, maybe never again. I don't know. I don't know what this is going to be."

A woman came up to me while we were on break and said, "If you have it in Orlando, I'll pay for the conference."

Whoa! That was a tremendous offer, so we started planning it for Orlando in 2017. Then the woman who'd made that offer unexpectedly passed away from an aggressive form of breast cancer. Her close friend, who was very involved in the prolife movement in Florida, came to me. "That doesn't change anything," she said. "We're still doing this. We'll do it in her honor. We're going to make this go forward." So, the conference has become an annual event, and God has generously seen to it that the resources are always available for us to continue.

Interestingly, we've had some reporters from the secular press attend each year. The first year, in Dallas, a reporter attended from a well-read news source usually highly critical of prolife efforts. I was concerned she'd write a negative report, though I wondered how since we were talking about being loving and reaching out to all people. I was delighted that it ended up being a pretty decent article for us. Then in 2018, we had a gal come from a popular online news source known for its liberal leanings. She spoke to me about all the sponsors and vendors that were set up. "Abby," she said, "I walked in here, and this conference is so beautiful. If this is what the prolife movement was, everyone would be prolife. What you're doing is really rebranding the prolife movement."

I thought back to the old (sadly accurate) image of prolife protests. On my first day working at the Planned Parenthood clinic, a man dressed as the grim reaper, scythe and all, loomed over a crowd bearing ugly signs. Yes, the prolife movement needs to be rebranded. I take that role pretty seriously.

I've seen over the years what happens when prolifers operate in isolation from one another, unaware of what God has done and is doing in our midst as individuals and as a whole. I've come to realize that all too often not only are we unaware of the great good God is doing in the battle for life, but we are also unaware of what God is doing in the hearts of our sisters and brothers in our cause. This unawareness causes divisions to rise up. Misunderstandings abound about one another's motives and methods. Criticism, judgment, and finger-pointing sneak into our hearts and our rhetoric.

The simple truth is, we have an enemy. And I'm not talking about a political leader or party. I'm talking about an enemy who operates in the spiritual dimension. An enemy who, in the end, knows he will lose the war but is bent on taking down as many of us with him as he can. An enemy who loves for the culture of death to permeate our world and loves to splinter God's people. An enemy who celebrates when misunderstanding, resentment, and bitterness divide us. "For our struggle is not against flesh and blood, but against the rulers, against the authorities, against the powers of this dark world and against the spiritual forces of evil in the heavenly realms" (Ephesians 6:12).

Therefore, it is critical that we permeate our efforts, our motives, and our methods with the outlandish mercy of God. Let the culture look at us and see God's mercy reflected. That's what happens when we come out of the saltshaker and into the world.

But because of his great love for us, God, who is rich in mercy, made us alive with Christ even when we were dead in transgressions—it is by grace you have been saved.

Ephesians 2:4–5

14

SPECIAL DELIVERY

This story begins in 2016. September 4, 2016, to be exact, and not in the United States but in Italy. Doug and I were there on pilgrimage for the canonization of Mother Teresa in Rome. Attending that was a major moment on my life's timeline. And it was on that trip that we felt moved to try to conceive our next child. In case you're trying to do the math, yes, by then we had five children. Grace was approaching her tenth birthday, Alex his fourth, Luke was three, Carter had just turned two, and Jude was nearly a year and a half.

Back in 2014, when we discovered I was pregnant with Carter, our fourth child, we didn't want to tell anybody. And we found that a sad place to be. Another child was something that we'd hoped for, that we were actively trying for, and yet we didn't want to tell people because we didn't want to hear their comments. Even so, once the news was out, hear them we did.

"What are you doing?"

"Why are you having so many kids?"

"You do know this can be prevented, right?"

Often these comments were delivered with overtones of disapproval and disappointment. Sadly, it's not unusual for me to hear the same experience from other couples with large families. They say, "We were afraid to tell our parents. We were afraid to tell our friends. We thought they would disapprove—and they did."

I grew up an only child, so for my parents, the idea of having a big family was foreign, maybe even difficult to understand. We didn't even tell my parents I was pregnant with Carter until I was probably about twelve weeks along. And Carter was only our fourth. It's not like we were the Duggars, with twenty kids. Our fourth! That's not that many. It used to be common; in fact, my mom was one of four kids.

But the disapproval of others caused no second thoughts on our part. Doug and I were totally of one mind on this. In our hearts, children are a tremendous blessing, and we love the dynamics of a large family. We love calling ourselves "open to life." We finally had to simply accept that many of our friends and family had a hard time understanding that. When I'm tempted to be frustrated by negative comments about the size of our family, I remind myself that it gives me an opportunity to exercise mercy.

We visited Assisi as part of our trip to Italy and loved it. This is how Doug described that day's events on his Facebook page:

After lunch, we wandered into a pretty cool mom-and-pop shop that sold lots of artwork, local trinkets, and some other cool stuff. We ended up buying some art and when we were checking out, I noticed some baptismal gowns hanging behind the counter. I pointed them out to Abby and said "Hey, if we end up conceiving here on our trip, it would be really cool to have one made in Italy . . . kinda like the baby."

I thought it was a great idea, so we bought the gown.[1]

Shortly after our return to the States, I knew I was pregnant, and a pregnancy test confirmed it. A few weeks later, I was at an event out of state and started bleeding pretty heavily. *I'm having a miscarriage!* I thought, and shot off a text to my doctor. "I'm so sorry to hear that," he texted back. "Come to the office as soon as you get back."

From the airport, I stopped at home only long enough to pick up Doug and then headed straight to the doctor's office. I walked in sure that I was going to hear, "We're so sorry, but . . ."

The prolife OB-GYN office I go to is a nonprofit attached to a pregnancy center. It's set up that way so any women who come in during a crisis pregnancy are able to see a physician, have an ultrasound, and then, if they choose, continue receiving care through that OB-GYN practice.

The ultrasound room has a huge monitor on the wall. That's because they really want the pregnant women to be able to see their baby clearly. We know that when a woman sees her baby on an ultrasound monitor, she is 85 percent more likely to choose life over abortion. The ultrasound is a powerful tool against the enemy. After all, it was an ultrasound that changed my mind about abortion. I went in that day expecting to hear the worst. I lay back onto the table feeling very nervous, and the technician smeared the cold gel onto my belly and began to move the abdominal probe around while I watched the screen. As soon as she started, I looked at the big monitor and gasped. I had viewed enough ultrasounds to know what I was seeing: two sacs. I must have scared the technician, because she immediately pulled up the probe, looked at me, and said, "Did you see that?"

And I scared Doug as well, who said, "What?"

"Yes," I answered the tech.

"Are you ready to see it again?"

"I don't know." And I didn't. Because suddenly so many uncertainties were in play. Was I carrying twins? Was I losing them? Both? Only one? There just seemed to be so much risk. But we couldn't *not* do the ultrasound, so the tech put the probe back onto my abdomen. And as she targeted certain areas and occasionally pushed down on my belly, I started saying, over and over, "Oh my word, oh my word . . ."

I could see their heartbeats. Two of them, actively beating, each in its own little chest in its own little sac. So, I knew they were alive. But contrary to what you might expect, I didn't necessarily feel real jazzed about it. Instead, I felt panicked. It was as if one panic—that I might be miscarrying—was transformed into a different kind.

"Oh my word, oh my word, oh my word."

Poor Doug. "What's going on?" he asked, because he'd been totally confused by the whole interaction so far and didn't know what he was looking at on the big monitor.

"There are two," I said.

"You mean like . . . two babies?"

"Yes."

Doug's reaction was entirely different from mine. He was immediately elated. "*Wow!* This is amazing!" He was as excited as if this were our very first baby.

Meanwhile, I was lying there saying, "No. I have one at a time. One! I don't have two at a time." It was not a joke, and not a casual response. The panic I felt was steadily growing as I watched the image.

We listened to the heartbeats—always a high point for an expectant couple. But even that didn't give me the slightest sense of excitement. Instead, I felt worried. Overwhelmed. You may be thinking, *But it was your choice! You were trying to get pregnant. Why the second thoughts now, when it was too late anyway?* And you're right. It wasn't an accident. It was deliberate. I had five kids at home, but of course I had known that when we decided to try again. What I *hadn't* known, though, was that I was going to end up pregnant with twins, and it just seemed to me in those initial moments that having two newborns at home with five other kids made it a whole new ball game—and not in a positive sense.

One of the first things that crossed my mind was, *How do I breastfeed two babies?* Because when my other kids were infants, I have to confess that I hated breastfeeding. I did it but did not enjoy it. Many moms love it, I know. But up until that point, I had not been one of them—and now to have not one but two to breastfeed at the same time? How does one even *do* that? Then more of the less happy memories from my previous pregnancies and births came rushing back: postpartum depression, weight gain that was hard to lose afterward, and others. And all while I was still lying there with the ultrasound probe pressing on my belly! I thought, *I don't know how to do this.*

My doctor came in. Of course, he was thrilled. "First," he said, "I don't think you need to worry about the bleeding. It looks like you have a little subchorionic hemorrhage. And that's common with twins. It's actually a sign of a healthy pregnancy."

Was I even hearing all of that good news? No, I was not. I was just lying there like a lump on the table. The tech was still moving the wand across my belly so that the doctor could see what was happening inside and take some measurements. The doctor kept saying things like, "Everything is great. Everything looks perfect."

And like a true neurotic, at this point I was feeling not only panicked because I was carrying twins but also guilty because I knew I should be excited. I'm a prolife speaker! I should be super thrilled about having two babies. And, of course, I was glad they were okay—but that relief was overshadowed by everything else going on in my head: the panic, the shock, and the guilt.

My emotions boiled over when they finished the ultrasound. I sat up and started crying. "I can't have two!" I said. "I don't know how to have two babies."

It was a sweet moment, because I had Doug on one side of me, with his arm around me, and Dr. K. on the other side, also with his arm around me. Dr. K. said, "Abby, you can do this! God has given you this. He knows you can handle it. You're a great mom."

As he was talking, I kept thinking, *Oh yeah, it's just great! But they're not coming out of YOUR body. You're not growing them. You're not going to have to go through HG with not one but two babies in your womb.* (HG is hyperemesis gravidarum. If you've never heard of or experienced it, first of all, you're lucky, and second, just think of it as morning sickness on steroids. And yes, I'd had it during my previous pregnancies and figured I would get it this time too—and I did.) *Sure. This all seems wonderful to you.*

They handed me the ultrasound pictures, and I walked out muttering, "No! No! This cannot be happening." One of the client advocates for the pregnancy center, a woman about my mom's age who I knew, was walking down the hallway toward us as we walked out. I had seen her as we were coming in and told her, "I think I may be having a miscarriage."

She had said, "I'm going to be praying. Please come let me know."

Now she said, "Well? What did you find out?" I broke down crying again but not for the reason she first assumed. "It's twins," I said. I didn't say, "It's twins!" like I was excited. My attitude was, "It's twins and it's horrible."

She hugged me while I cried. Finally, she pulled me away from her, with her hands on my shoulders, and said, "Abby, you can do this. You were made for this." That was what I needed to hear right at that moment. I guess the praying she'd been doing while I was in the ultrasound room had helped. By the time I left, I felt better. She was just the right person to deliver that message. I didn't need someone my own age, no matter how positive—I needed a mom figure. She was celebrating even in the midst of my panic, and coming from her, I didn't find it objectionable. In fact, it made me feel a bit confident.

Doug and I decided to stop for Mexican food on our way home, and once we were seated, we couldn't stop laughing. "Well, we prayed for a baby," I said, "and we go to Rome and come home with two. We shouldn't be surprised—after all, we were there to celebrate the canonization of a saint, and that requires a miracle or two."

Next, we sent a video to my parents, who knew we were trying to have yet another baby and thought we were nuts. In the video, Alex is holding the ultrasound picture. And I say, "What is that?" And he says something like, "Oh, it's babies." And I say, "Where are those babies?" And he says,

"In Mommy's tummy." And I say, "How many babies are there?" He says, believe it or not, "Six." I laugh and say, "No, not six." Then he gets it right: "Two." And then Doug puts his head into the video and says, "Yeah, that's right—we're having twins. So, we expect a callback soon."

After my mom watched the video—but without really listening to what Doug said at the end—she turned to Dad and said, "Well, they're having another baby." Then she thought for a moment and said, "Wait—did they say *two* babies?" She watched the video again and said, "Mike! They're having twins!" My dad is a twin himself.

So, my mom, who generally isn't an excitable person, called and said, "Did you say you're pregnant with twins?"

"Yes."

"Oh my! There are two!" This was, I was aware, a three-way conversation, because she was talking to me but also relaying everything I said to my dad.

Were my parents worried? Sure. Their daughter was pregnant with twins. They knew that meant it was a higher-risk pregnancy, and add to that the fact that I was over thirty-five. My safety was their first concern, and their questions that came next showed it: "Are you feeling okay? Are the babies okay?"

"Yes, everything is fine."

"How far along are you?"

"Seven weeks," I said, swallowing back the panic rising in my chest.

AS SOON AS I FOUND OUT I was pregnant with the twins, partially in an effort to counteract the panic I felt at the thought of having two newborns at the same time, I began to pray for two things. Two *big* things. First, I prayed that I would love breastfeeding. As I said, I was never one of those women who loved it from the first time they held a baby to their breast and felt them latch on, and then continued to love it just as much with each child. Sure, I breastfed my kids. But I can't say it was my favorite part of the motherhood experience. I wanted that to change. I wanted to breastfeed these twins joyfully.

And second, I prayed for time with them—and with the rest of my kids—without any distractions. If you think, given the pattern of my life, that was asking a lot, you're right. Abby, the reforming workaholic, was seldom content to just stay home. I was always on a mission. I felt a drive to get back onto the speaking circuit, into the office, or on the phone to plan upcoming events, back to writing my next talk for my next conference, back before the cameras or in front of the microphone, and so on. Yes, I'd made strides in this area, especially since adopting Jude. And yes, I missed my kids when I was traveling and couldn't wait to get home to them. But once I was home from a trip, I always felt a strong pull to get back onto the circuit again. So, I prayed that somehow, someway, I would find a way to spend time with Doug and our kids without distractions, without the constant pull to read emails, write speeches, and take calls. To just revel in being a mom.

Like I said—two *big* prayers!

IF YOU'RE KEEPING TRACK, we now had two babies on the way—and one very cool baptismal gown from Assisi. One. So, unless we planned to hurry the babies out of and into the gown, taking turns with it as each one's turn at the font came, we were one baptismal gown short. And with no plans to rush over to Assisi to pick up another one, we were in a pickle. We had to pick from the following choices:

- Let one of the twins be baptized in the very cool Italian gown and the other in a gown from some other undoubtedly less cool place, like, say, Macy's.
- Find some way to pick up another matching gown from Assisi.
- Give the Italian gown we loved away and buy *two* new but admittedly less exciting and meaningful gowns.

THE PREGNANCY WENT WELL. They were super healthy babies. But as you can imagine with twins, I got huge. I didn't think I could get any bigger, and then I did. Having twins does not do good things to the shape and fitness of your body, especially if you already have loose skin on your belly from previous pregnancies. I was thankful that, with God's help, I had already worked through that self-image issue to some extent after my past pregnancies, because if I hadn't, I think that could have thrown me into despair and taken the joy out of having those two babies.

My experience with multiple pregnancies wasn't the only thing that necessitated my working on my body image issues. More than once I'd heard unwelcome commentary on my weight through social media, giving me practice at exercising mercy toward those with unkind things to say. These experiences had sensitized me to the body image problems that women have in our society.

I talked once with a girl who was scheduled to have an abortion. The primary reason she didn't want to carry the baby to term was because of the effects the pregnancy might have on her body. "I'm twenty years old," she said, "and I don't want to have stretch marks all over my body. I want to be able to go on spring break and wear a bikini."

Many people would say, "That's ridiculous and selfish." And all of us, at least on the prolife side, applaud the decision she finally made not to have an abortion. Even so, those of us who have borne children look at the effects on our own bodies and understand her concerns. We know how negative body image experiences can be emotionally traumatic. I didn't consider her attitude to be selfish. I found it very honest. But I also knew it was something she could work through.

In the process of carrying my babies, I actually became grateful for the stretch marks and loose skin. They were, I realized, a reminder of a gift. Many women long for the experience of giving birth and would gladly accept stretch marks and loose skin as a reasonable price to pay for it. In my case, the opportunity to deliver children was freely given. That perspective helped me see my changing body, my *mom* body, as something to be grateful for. Things aren't in the same place they were when I was twenty years old, like the young woman I had counseled, but that's okay. I'd birthed and breastfed four children. Had that taken a toll on my body? You bet it had. And that was all right.

I WAS ALMOST thirty-nine weeks when I delivered. And by all means, it was a special delivery!

Here's something you won't hear very often: I love being in labor. I love having babies—not just *having had* them but the process of *having* them. I don't mind the pain. I think it's wonderful how our bodies know what to do. Time to get it out? Our bodies instinctively know how to push. I know I sound like someone whose labors must have been relatively easy. Other than my first delivery with Grace, which was hard, it's true that babies come fast and easy for me.

The morning of May 15, a Monday, we got up early because we had to be at the hospital before 6:30. The kids were up, although, of course, they'd be staying home. Our friend Heather was staying with them. I was so nervous leaving that morning! That was the first time I'd ever been nervous about having a baby. But this time was different— not only was I having twins, but I just knew that I was going to have to have a C-section with one of them. My doctor had assured me, "Everything's great. Baby A is head down. Baby B is breech, but that's not a problem. I can do a breech extraction. No big deal." I wasn't confident that the breech extraction was "no big deal," and I felt that something was going to go wrong. Could it have been mother's intuition?

Everything went well at first. They induced my labor in the operating room, as they usually prefer to do with twins, so that in the event something does go wrong, they're already set up for a C-section. Lucy, the first, came quickly, as my babies usually do. In fact, by the time they got me to the OR, Lucy was coming! I pushed twice, and she shot out like a rocket. I was so excited! *Okay,* I wondered, *when do I start pushing for Maggie?* But I didn't feel that intense pressure to push, and when I asked my doctor about it, he said, "Well,

I'm sure she's breech." So, he reached up into my uterus and tried to pull her out.

In actuality, Maggie wasn't in a breech position but a transverse position—diagonal—which meant the doctor couldn't reach her feet. He dug around up there for about ten minutes, trying to get a grip that would allow him to guide her out. By that time, the cord was slipping out. Because of that, he was concerned about cord prolapse, which could cause the baby to lose oxygen.

"Abby," he said very calmly, "I need to get this baby out. Quickly."

When I arrived that morning, I'd been very nervous about the possibility of a C-section; however, when the moment actually came, I felt complete peace. "Get her out," I said. "I don't care how you have to slice me open. Just get my baby out."

The worst part was that Doug, who'd been with me up to that point, was whisked out because it had now turned into an emergency C-section. I could see how worried he was, could see the fear on his face. And I didn't want him to worry because I was completely calm.

The *other* worst part was that, even though they'd given me an epidural, it wasn't working. In fact, after my first two deliveries, epidurals just didn't work on me anymore. So as Doug was being escorted out, the OR was frantic—everyone was scrambling because that baby had to come out fast. The drape was coming off, my arms were being strapped down, and the OR personnel were ripping open packages of sterile supplies, causing wrappings to fly through the air.

Knowing that there might be a problem with the epidural, they shot another intravenous dose into my spinal to see if that would help. Almost immediately, Dr. K. lowered his hands to my abdomen (where I couldn't see, of course) and said, "Tell me what you feel right now."

"It feels like a scalpel going into my skin."

"Okay," he said, "it's not working."

No, it's really not.

The anesthesiologist instantly prepped me to deliver Maggie under general anesthesia. The last thing I remember before I went under is Dr. K. peeking over the drape and saying, "Don't worry. If you get pregnant again, you can still have a vaginal delivery after this."

I laughed out loud. And I thought, *We're thinking about future deliveries now? How about we just get this baby out first, okay?* And then I was out.

"WHERE'S MAGGIE?" I mumbled as I struggled to come out of the anesthesia.

"She's fine. She's healthy," a nurse said. "Do you want to see them?"

I not only wanted to see my babies—I wanted to breast-feed them. I had never felt that urge with any of my other newborns.

I was terribly groggy and in a lot of pain. When you have a planned C-section, they typically give you pain meds before the surgery so that afterward the pain is under control. But because mine had been an emergency C-section, there wasn't time to give me the pain meds. When I woke up, my body felt the full brunt of what had just happened. But at that point I didn't care. I just wanted to feed those babies. By the time a bit more of the grogginess had worn off, the first strong memory I have is of the nurses bringing me both babies. I was actually able to tandem feed them—both at one time. That was cool. And it was clearly an answer to one of my prayers.

At some point my parents came into the room, and I remember my dad crying a bit. I think he was worried because I didn't look good. Usually after I have a baby, I'm great. I'm up walking around. I have makeup on. But this time, I'd just been through a major surgery, and getting up to stand before the mirror and put makeup on was not an option. I'm sure I looked like death warmed over.

Then my in-laws came in, but I must have been getting sleepy because I only vaguely remember that. Not long after they arrived, the nurses shooed them all out because everyone was packed into the tiny recovery room.

Shortly afterward, the hospital staff moved me and the babies to a postpartum room, where we spent the rest of the week. It was a very healing time for me. I loved every minute of being with my two new ones. And here's a newsflash—*I had no desire to get back to work!*

Only God could produce that kind of heart change in me!

To illustrate this amazing difference, you should know that the day after I had Carter in August 2014, I Skyped into a legislative conference call—from my hospital bed. It wasn't just that they needed me—I *wanted* to do it.

But this time, I didn't even want to look at my email. I wanted nothing to do with work. I just wanted to sit and look at my babies and feed them. So that's what I did.

Because of the C-section, my hospital stay was longer than for a normal delivery. I delivered on Monday and didn't leave until Friday, which was great. I needed it. I needed the time to let my body recover. I liked having nurses there. I liked having my food delivered. I liked being pampered. I was in no hurry to leave.

Until Friday, and then I thought, *Okay, time to go home.* We have two recliners in our bedroom. When we got home, I went and sat in my recliner, and with only a couple of exceptions, that's where I sat for three months. I breastfed those babies and pumped, and Doug brought me food. That's really all I did.

Except for the third weekend in June. That's when we have the Pro-Life Women's Conference. It's the one I started in 2016, so I felt I needed to be there. I loaded up the twins, a month old by that time, and the three of us went to Orlando for the conference, accompanied by friends who traveled with me to help with the babies. As usual, Doug stayed home with the older kids.

At the conference, I had very little I needed to do. The first year, I emceed the conference, but I didn't that year. The conference began on a Friday night, and I introduced a panel of former abortion workers who had come through ATTWN. I moderated the discussion, and that concluded my responsibilities at that year's conference. Stepping away from all the roles I'd played the year before as conference director gave me a chance to see what I had created, a chance to observe—almost as an outsider—what worked well and what didn't.

At the conference we have a mother's room—a private area set up within the conference hall where women can pump or feed and change their babies comfortably. We have snacks and rocking chairs, a fridge for breast milk. Changing tables. Everything a breastfeeding mom would need. And for most of the conference, that's where I sat and fed my babies. And everybody got to see them. It was fun.

When I came home, I did nothing else until August. For the first time in my life, I had no desire to work. I just wanted to focus on my babies and my other kids. So, the summer of 2017 turned out to be really, really good.

I'd never stayed away from work for so long. Usually the summer months are fairly slow for speaking and by August I'm chomping at the bit with an overwhelming sense of "I've got to get out of here." I'm usually ready to go back to work and get back on the road. But in 2017, I cried when the first event came that required me to travel and leave my babies and the rest of my kids behind. I so loved having them surround me all spring and summer.

I can't emphasize it enough: this was a huge defining moment in my motherhood.

This was also clearly the answer to my second prayer—that I would be able to have uninterrupted "mom" time with these babies and the rest of my kids. What a blessing it was that the two things I prayed for throughout my pregnancy were both answered in positive and powerful ways. I see those answers to my prayers as more special deliveries of good gifts from God.

LUCY AND MAGGIE were baptized on December 31, 2017. Originally, you'll recall, we had only one baptismal gown from Assisi, Italy, because at the time we bought it, we never even considered the possibility of having twins. We resolved that dilemma in a very twenty-first-century way: social media. Doug mentioned our problem on Facebook—and in no time, people were offering to help. In the end, it was Angie Hass who replied on Doug's Facebook page. She explained that she was going to Assisi to visit her boyfriend who was there for school, and to our amazement she asked the name of the shop and offered to buy us a second identical gown. Sure enough, before long, Angie shipped us a matching baptismal gown. Another special delivery! So, Lucy and Maggie were presented for baptism in their wonderful matching gowns from Assisi.

> I love the LORD, for he heard my voice;
> he heard my cry for mercy.
> Because he turned his ear to me,
> I will call on him as long as I live.
>
> Psalm 116:1–2

15

THE ECHO

knew I was in the right place . . . ," the first chapter of this book began.

That's also how I felt on March 18, 2019, as I sat in Grauman's Chinese Theater, my eyes glued to the movie screen as I watched the premier of *Unplanned*. Doug sat to my right and our now thirteen-year-old daughter, Grace, sat to my left. I was mesmerized by the film, awed that the Lord had brought it to pass. I remembered my tumultuous emotions on the film set so many months before. Tonight was different—my overwhelming feeling now was joy: *God will use this movie to save lives around the globe*, I thought.

I kept my eye on Grace, wanting to be sensitive to any sign that the movie might be too much for her. Through much of the film she seemed fine, including the horrendous scenes of the ultrasound and of the medication abortion. Then the scene opened of "me" staring at the pregnancy test in the restroom at work. My supervisor comes out of a stall, sees the test, and offers to "take care of that"[1] for me. Grace, of course, realized that the baby I was carrying at that point was her. She tensed up and began to fidget.

The scene shifts to a conversation between me and the supervisor, who says, "And you're committed to carrying this pregnancy to term?"[2]

"I am," I answer.[3] The supervisor, clearly displeased with my response, proceeds to apply some not-so-subtle pressure to not spend my precious time parenting when I could be investing it, instead, at the clinic. I defend my decision while assuring my boss that I wouldn't allow mothering to interfere with my work or dedication.

Grace, I noticed, wiped a few tears from her eyes but showed no signs of wanting to leave. She was fine through the rest of the movie.

Later, in the lobby of the theater after the crowds had cleared, Doug and I said goodbye to Grace, who would be going home with my parents while Doug and I headed to the airport to catch a red-eye flight to New York for media interviews. Grace wrapped her arms around me and squeezed hard. I squeezed her back, then stepped away to make eye contact.

"Are you sad?" I asked.

"No. I'm thankful," Grace said.

"Thankful?"

"Yes," she said. "I didn't know until tonight that you had to negotiate for my life."

I was stunned. Grace had realized for the first time that I'd been pressured to abort her by someone who'd held considerable influence in my life, yet I had chosen life for her, and she was thankful. My heart swelled with thankfulness as well. I couldn't imagine my life without my precious daughter. I'll always hear the echo of her precious voice saying, "I'm thankful."

"IN THE RIGHT place" was also how I felt just six weeks after the premier on Saturday, May 4, 2019—that I was in *exactly* the right place and was honored to be there. I was climbing into a mobile medical unit positioned in one of the five busiest intersections on the planet—New York's Times Square, the Crossroads of the World. My precious preborn son, Fulton, merely three weeks from his due date, was about to pose for a picture—a live 4D ultrasound—that would be projected on three massive digital screens in the square and broadcast live via livestream and radio.

It was the week before Mother's Day, and the event at which Fulton would be the guest of honor was called Alive from NY: See Life Clearly. Focus on the Family and the March for Life Education and Defense Fund, the organizers, had prolife speakers and music lined up for a ninety-minute program. I was to be the final guest speaker. But Fulton would be the star of the show before I spoke.

The idea to stage this public celebration of life was born in response to the fact that the sanctity of human life was under siege in multiple states that spring, with many elected officials advocating for unrestricted abortion even up to the moment of birth. The original plan for the event called for my third-trimester ultrasound to be broadcast on the renowned giant billboard screens in Times Square. Sadly, the Times Square billboard owners denied us the use of their screens for this purpose, but that didn't stop prolifers from bringing in the three jumbo digital screens now in place.

Times Square, almost always loud and boisterous, throbbed with noise that afternoon. An estimated twenty thousand prolife supporters pressed into the areas surrounding the stage and screens, and about two thousand protesters gathered as well.[4] I heard in conversations backstage that some of the protesters had brought large drums to pound to try to drown out our sound system, but they were no match for the thousands of decibels our three sound stages were blasting into the surrounding neighborhoods. Evidently the protesters dispersed and were heard from no more.

Given the noise of the crowd, I was surprised by the hush as I stepped into the medical van provided by ICU Mobile—like an RV—and closed the door behind me. Despite the throngs of people right outside, I felt like we had quiet privacy. The female technician gave me a warm welcome and invited me to climb up on the examination table. I'd had tons of experience with ultrasounds, given all my pregnancies, so I bared my belly in preparation for the warm gel. But I'd never seen a 4D image this far along into my pregnancy before and I was excited, wondering how much detail I'd be able to make out.

The next thing I knew, I was watching Fulton's fuzzy black-and-white image in 2D, which is the starting point of capturing the 4D image. Then there he was, in 4D, in color. It was like looking at a 3D photo. Only better! I could make out his little lips and his head resting peacefully on the placenta like it was a pillow. He seemed to be sleeping. The technician, in her gentle feminine voice, narrated for me and for the audience as she shifted the probe to show various views. He stretched and yawned and arched his head back. I loved this little guy so much already. I just wanted to reach out to the screen and cuddle him, and then I smiled at the thought that I already had him cuddled in my womb.

Then, finally, "Let's listen to the heartbeat," she said. And suddenly the matchless sound of a heartbeat thumped with a quick rhythm. My heart leaped, and at the same time applause and cheers erupted from the crowd outside as Fulton's heartbeat echoed through the streets.

And in that sweet sound, I heard the echo of God's mercy.

UNDESERVED FAVOR AND COMPASSION. Surely the Lord had poured that into my life in abundance. God was giving me—a woman who'd sacrificed two babies on the altar of convenience and influenced countless other women to do the same—my eighth child. Now that child's heartbeat was being heard, applauded, and cheered on the streets of Manhattan as evidence for the value and sanctity of the life of the unborn.

A heartbeat is the universal sound of life. I was told by some who were out in the square that day that when the applause faded, a hush fell over the crowd. They simply listened. Times Square—quieted by the sound of a baby's heartbeat. Imagine!

As I write now, I think about all the ways I hear the echo of God's mercy in my life. I hear it in the laughter of my children and in the voice of my husband. I hear it in the voices of my parents. In this book, I've shared with you that I heard it sitting in church, calling me more deeply into motherhood. And in the desperate crying of my name backstage when Annette—my first "client" and my inspiration to start ATTWN—first reached out for me. Today, her life totally transformed, Annette is a stay-at-home mom to her five children.

I hear God's mercy in each of the voices of our staff members when they are talking with and serving our clients. And I hear it in the stories of our ATTWN quitters. A memory of

Adrienne suddenly surfaces. In January 2017, a group of us from ATTWN were attending the March for Life in Washington, DC, and I'd invited Adrienne to come with us. She was still doing so much healing, so I said, "We don't have to tell anybody who you are, or even that you're a former abortion worker. We would just like you to experience it with us."

But she said, "I'm okay with telling my story now. And the reason is that I feel so supported. I know now that I'm not alone." And so, the 2017 March for Life became the first time since her arrest that she "went public" with her story. One of the places she did that was at the headquarters of the Family Research Council. Every year they ask me and others in the prolife world to come and say a few words to those attending a pre-march conference. The general theme that year concerned bringing the prolife movement into the digital age, and most of the others who spoke talked about how they developed their websites, used social media, and so on. It was useful information, but as I wondered before the conference what I should say, I found myself thinking less about the technology itself, which I know little about anyway, and more about how our online presence as prolifers sometimes sends the wrong message.

And so, like a true Debbie Downer, when my turn came, I got up and said, "You know, over my years in the prolife movement, I don't think we've policed our own movement well online. Instead, there's a lot of keyboard courage—people saying things about someone else that we would never say to their face. And this is not going unnoticed. People are watching. *Women* are watching—women who have had abortions and who are now looking for healing. And what they often read online from the prolife movement is that they are *baby killers* and *murderers*.

"Those women are watching you. And they're listening. Our harsh, judgmental words are impeding their ability to heal. And we will be held responsible for that. Imagine the woman who is pregnant and confused about abortion, who thinks abortion is one option and may be the best one because it takes care of her problem—and her boyfriend's. That woman goes online looking for information about abortion. What she finds is prolifers saying, 'Well, she wouldn't have this problem if she weren't such a slut' or 'She should have kept her legs closed.' Those women are listening carefully to your words. They're watching how we love. Or how we don't."

Then I talked about the Gosnell case. "I remember hearing prolifers say they were praying for the workers in that clinic to go to hell. Saying that they hoped someone would stick a knife in the back of the head of each of the women who worked there. When you called them murderers—when you said that they weren't worthy of forgiveness, that God had forsaken them—they were listening. One woman, in particular, was listening."

Then I called Adrienne up to the front, introduced her, and let her speak. She was transparent and, once again, like at the retreat, very moved. She was in tears, and soon so was everyone else. Adrienne and I then took our seats, hoping our words would be taken to heart. People were fascinated by her story, of course, just as they are with all things Gosnell. But when Adrienne tells her story, it isn't just a confession of wrongs committed or a historical recounting. It's a moving testimony. An inspiring statement of her faith.

What I said at that gathering was and still is true—we *haven't* policed ourselves well. The prolife movement too often views those of us who have come out of the abortion industry in terms of who we were in our past. Where we worked. What we did. Who we worked with—like Kermit Gosnell. The movement too seldom views us in terms of who we are *now*, what we're doing *now*. And that causes us to think we're never going to get out from under the used-to-work-in-an-abortion-clinic label.

I think one reason the prolife movement has been quite judgmental toward the men and women who work in the abortion industry is that we think they *want* to be there. We think they know full well what they're getting into and what they're doing, and that they love doing it. But in my many years of working first inside the industry and then working outside with current and former abortion workers, I have *not* found that to be true. Oh, sure, some are fully knowledgeable and fully committed. But those people are primarily in management. Like *me*. I loved my job at Planned Parenthood, especially once I got into management. That seems to be the turning point for people—once they make it into management, especially if they've worked their way up, they're all in. But for the most part, the average workers were naïvely unaware at the outset and are sadly disillusioned after time in the job. This is one reason our postcard outreach to them has been so effective.

AS I LAY ON THE EXAM TABLE in the medical van in Times Square, belly bared, listening to Fulton's heartbeat to the soundtrack of the cheers of thousands of people, I felt emotions course through me that I struggled to name. I'm still struggling to find words for how I felt then and how I feel as I'm writing to you about it now. Vulnerable. Exposed yet safe. And oddly enough, *responsible.* Responsible to make the most of this moment God provided, to find the message of the moment and share it with a world so beleaguered by the never-ending onslaught of an enemy who loves death and destruction and wants to wield it to wound our already hurting world.

So, hear me as I implore you to understand that it's vitally important that we encourage one another to put away our words of anger and hate and speak instead in echoes of God's fierce mercy. That's the heartbeat of this book. It's why I urged you to be willing to pray dangerous prayers. It's why I challenged you to consider that God loves the victimizer as much as the victim, and why I suggested that when you see the evil in others, you remember you are looking into a mirror of the unvanquished evil that still lurks in your own heart. We must *learn* to echo God's mercy—because it is not natural to our sinful hearts. I called you to make a choice to take your stand, even when it puts you at risk. I sought to inspire you to see others through that lens of mercy and to seek out your deeper purpose. Through the stories of Jude's adoption and the birth of the twins, I hoped to help you focus on the bond that God our Father enjoys sharing with us and to appreciate the ways he pours dreams into our hearts and then fulfills them. And in "Out of the Saltshaker," I invited you to join me, to leap willingly from the isolation of your own subculture, the saltshaker, and throw yourself wholeheartedly into the lives and hearts of the people in our culture.

Throwing yourself into the culture may very well mean being willing to feel uncomfortable. In January 2017, the first-ever Women's March in Washington, DC, was held the day after the presidential inauguration. I decided to participate. First, I registered for ATTWN to have a display there as many other women's causes or organizations were going to do, but the organizers refused to allow us to participate in that way. (I can't say I was surprised.) I decided that I'd go instead as an individual, just as a woman, even though I knew Planned Parenthood was one of the event's biggest sponsors.

Not surprisingly, I got a lot of criticism from other pro-lifers for going, so I explained to people that wherever there are pro-abortion voices, there *must* also be voices of life. I realize that makes many people super uncomfortable, but it is, I believe, an important message for me to deliver. (You might say I have the gift of making people in prolife squirm. I'm okay with that. I'll gladly play that role because I feel called to it, especially as I take the message of this book to them.) If all we do is stay in our own little subculture—safe in our saltshaker—speaking only to each other, we aren't taking our *rightful place* as a voice in our culture.

A friend joined me at the Women's March, and we had a lot of authentic conversations with individual women. Conversations I believe could possibly be fruitful in the future. Memorable conversations that may cause some of the women we spoke with to think about the reasons we are prolife and believe in valuing and protecting the unborn. These are conversations that we never would have had if we had shoved a bullhorn in their faces.

I saw that method at work there, of course. I recall one prolife group with a bullhorn, and women on both sides were screaming and yelling back and forth at each other. As I observed this inflammatory interaction with sadness, I thought, *We have to figure out how to do this better.* James

3:17 tells us the wisest way to interact with culture: "But the wisdom that comes from heaven is first of all pure; then peace-loving, considerate, submissive, full of mercy and good fruit, impartial and sincere."

Yes. We must recognize that in all things that we do—whether we're attending a women's march or event or something sponsored by Planned Parenthood or whatever it is—we must show up with a heart of mercy, because we have to recognize that a huge number of the women in attendance may have had abortions. So they're angry. And behind their anger is hurt. But they don't recognize the difference. We have to be there to love them so they can see, and come to the realization on their own, that they are loved. By us. Because God loves them.

I realize that I am rubbing against the grain of many believers in making this statement, but I believe it with all my heart: It is time to bring an end to the mentality that we are in a culture war and it is our job to wipe out "the enemy." Those on the other side of abortion are not—I repeat, *are not*—our enemy. They are our mission field!

The real enemy is the prince of darkness. Sadly, he still roams this earth, determined to snatch as many into his twisted thinking as he can and take them with him to his doom. But he has *already lost the war*. His doom is certain and secure. We must remember that he does not own our culture! Not as long as we are in it. For when we call ourselves by the name of Christ—Christians—we must put aside our thirst to "win" the arguments in our culture on the issues of the day and instead work to win disciples into the body of Christ.

Always remember that Jesus already gave us our marching orders. He gave us our deeper purpose:

Then Jesus came to them and said, "All authority in heaven and on earth has been given to me. Therefore go and make disciples of all nations, baptizing them in the name of the Father and of the Son and of the Holy Spirit, and teaching them to obey everything I have commanded you. And surely I am with you always, to the very end of the age." (Matt. 28:18–20)

So, do that—go, make disciples, teach them the love of Jesus for them—and do so with fierce mercy. Live and love in such a way that God's mercy will echo from your life and your actions and into the streets, halls, homes, and hearts of our world.

Therefore, I urge you, brothers and sisters, in view of God's mercy, to offer your bodies as a living sacrifice, holy and pleasing to God—this is your true and proper worship.

Romans 12:1

ACKNOWLEDGMENTS

First, I must acknowledge the person who took on the ministry adventure of ATTWN with me, Jennie (Stone) MacGregor. When everyone thought I was crazy, you thought I was actually onto something, and you believed in the power of conversion. Thank you for being committed to this vision. I do not thank you for leaving your suitcase in the middle of the hotel room floor and almost causing me to break my neck in my middle-of-the-night bathroom break. I also do not thank you for throwing pillows at my head when you wanted me to stop snoring, scaring me half to death. But for everything else, I thank you from the bottom of my heart. You helped create this, and I sincerely couldn't have done it without you.

I remember when Doug and I first got married, we agreed to be part of a psychology student's research project because it paid fifty dollars and we were broke. We had to go to three sessions with this psychology student, and I was pregnant with Grace at the time. She asked us if we felt like having a baby would change our lives at all. Our reply? "Nope! We will make the baby fit around our schedule." Ha ha! We were the best parents *before* we had kids, weren't we, babe? During one of the sessions, I remember the gal saying that she saw us like music, one of us like the treble and the other like the bass. She said we had complementary personalities. I think that was her way of saying we were complete opposites. We used to laugh and quote that line sometimes. But it really is true. You keep me grounded, Doug. You are the better half of our home. I couldn't ask for a more amazing husband and father to our children. I have heard you say that you are my "soft spot to land," and that is so true. Thank you for that. Thank you for always being my most trusted advocate.

I have to thank my children for loaning me out to the world. Many of them are too young to understand the work I do. They just know that they miss their mom. I always pray that God will redeem the time lost, and I know he will. He does. I have to believe that my kids seeing their mom fight so hard for moms and their babies is doing some good. Grace always says, "Mom, when you die, I will take your place and be a prolife speaker." Um, thanks, honey. Let's not put me in the ground too quickly. Also, a huge thank-you to my parents and my in-loves for always helping with our kids and loving our family so well. We are blessed to have our parents nearby, which means our kids get to grow up close to their grandparents. We promise we are done.

A huge thank-you to Cindy Lambert for all her work on this book. I don't know how it is that you are able to navigate the stories of my life so well. I truly feel like God put us together all those years ago to help proclaim the message he has given me to say. What God allowed us to do with *Unplanned* has quite literally changed the world. That wouldn't have happened without you. You understand my thoughts and feelings in such a unique way. Thank you for saying yes to me and to the Holy Spirit, and for instinctively knowing that you need to send me a text every time you email me so that I pay attention to it.

Thank you to Wes Yoder and Gloria Leyda at Ambassador Speakers Bureau for representing me as my literary and speaking agents. I can honestly say I am represented by the very best. I mean, if your agent doesn't walk around barefoot in his office, then you clearly need to find a new one.

To my incredible travel guru, Emily Kinkade, you can blame me for your gray hairs.

Thank you to Baker Books for bringing this book to fruition. It has been such a joy to work with your team. From book design to editing to marketing, your professionalism has been appreciated. Thank you for working so hard to advance the message of Christ to the world. And thank you for your patience since I'm obviously terrible at meeting deadlines! You guys are the best.

To my ATTWN tribe: I no longer walk this road alone because of you. I don't know how I could ever express what that means to me. We have a shared grief. We have all seen things we shouldn't have seen. We have lived through a conversion experience that we wish we never would have had to experience in the first place. But we did it together. We are healing together. We are all different, yet so similar. We are strong. Beautiful. You have all made me more courageous. Thank you for trusting me. Thank you for trusting this ministry. I love you all so, so much.

I don't know of any organization that has a better staff than we do at ATTWN. Imagine a staff of almost thirty women who all get along, who love each other and have no drama. If that isn't a God thing, then I don't know what is! Thank you all for loving our clients so well. Thank you for working so hard for them. You are all like my sisters from another mister.

Thank you to the amazing attorneys and staff at the Thomas More Society who step forward to work with every ATTWN client who needs legal assistance. You help our clients rediscover their voice so they have the strength to go on with confidence. All those terrible lawyer jokes don't apply to you guys.

Finally, I must mention three priests. Father Frank Pavone, you were part of my story before I even left Planned Parenthood. I have to believe that all those nights that I watched you on EWTN were planting seeds of truth in my heart, even if I was yelling at you while you talked on the TV. You have loved me well over the years, and I thank you for always answering the phone when I call, day or night. Alex is blessed with an awesome godfather. Father Michael O'Connor, I'm not sure you recognize what a powerful influence you have been in my life. I know you have gone to bat for me many times. I know you have protected me. You have done it quietly, as you do. You baptized my children. You confirmed both Doug and me into the church. You gave me the Body and Blood of Jesus Christ for the very first time. You have been such a powerful force for healing in my life. I know I have not said it enough, but thank you for all you have done. To Father Paul Michael Piega, little did you know that the prayers you sent up as a university student for an abortion clinic director would follow you around for so many years! Be careful what you pray for. I am constantly thankful that the future of our church lies in the hands of amazing men like you. Thank you for your friendship, your pastoral counsel, and yes, for your obviously very powerful prayers.

God, thank YOU for your fierce mercy.

NOTES

Chapter 6 The Mirror

1. Conor Friedersdorf, "Why Dr. Kermit Gosnell's Trial Should Be a Front-Page Story," *The Atlantic*, April 12, 2013, https://www.theatlantic.com/national/archive/2013/04/why-dr-kermit-gosnells-trial-should-be-a-front-page-story/274944/.
2. Friedersdorf, "Why Dr. Kermit."
3. Friedersdorf, "Why Dr. Kermit."
4. Friedersdorf, "Why Dr. Kermit."

Chapter 9 A Deeper Purpose

1. Pope Francis, *Evangelii Gaudium*, quoted in Kevin Cotter, "A Summary of Evangelii Gaudium (Joy of the Gospel): Pope Francis' First Apostolic Exhortation," August 13, 2017, https://focusequip.org/a-summary-of-evangelii-gaudium-joy-of-the-gospel-pope-francis-first-apostolic-exhortation/.
2. Cindy Wooden, "A Summary of the Key Issues Raised by Pope in Evangelii Gaudium," November 26, 2013, https://catholicherald.co.uk/evangelii-gaudium-a-summary-of-the-key-issues-raised-by-pope/.
3. Wikipedia, s.v. *Evangelii gaudium*, accessed August 5, 2021, https://en.wikipedia.org/wiki/Evangelii_gaudium.

Chapter 11 Jude's Gift

1. Doug Johnson, "Adopting Jude: From Absolutely Not to Let's Do This!" April 27, 2021, *Doug on Tap*, http://www.dougontap.com/2015/05/adopting-jude-part-1/.

2. Johnson, "Adopting Jude."
3. Johnson, "Adopting Jude."

Chapter 14 Special Delivery

1. Doug Johnson (Doug on Tap), "Funny story about this baptismal gown . . . I think everyone knows by now that when Abby and I were in Rome for Mother Teresa's canonization, and that's when when the twins were conceived," Facebook, March 20, 2017, https://www.facebook.com/dougontap/photos/a.868824686470978/1465088440177930.

Chapter 15 The Echo

1. *Unplanned*, directed by Cary Solomon and Chuck Konzelman (Scottsdale, AZ: Pure Flix Entertainment, 2019), Blu-ray Disc.
2. *Unplanned*.
3. *Unplanned*.
4. Kevin McCullough, "ALIVE from New York: The Day Abortion Died," Townhall, May 5, 2019, https://townhall.com/columnists/kevin mccullough/2019/05/05/alive-from-new-york-the-day-abortion-died -n2545863.

Abby Johnson has always been fiercely determined to help women in need. This desire is what led Abby to a career with Planned Parenthood and then caused her to flee the organization, becoming an outspoken advocate for the prolife movement. Today, Abby travels the globe sharing her story, educating the public on prolife issues, advocating for the unborn, and reaching out to abortion clinic staff who still work in the industry. She is the founder of ProLove Ministries and also And Then There Were None, a ministry designed to assist abortion clinic workers in transitioning out of the industry. To date, this ministry has helped over 550 workers leave the abortion industry. Abby lives in Texas with her husband and eight precious children.

Connect with

▶ @AbbyJohnson

🐦 @AbbyJohnson

f @AbbyJohnson

📷 @prolifeabbyjohnson

Learn more at **abbyj.com**

Prolove Ministries

Promoting new ideas to solve old problems by creating life-affirming projects, supporting the launch of new organizations, and bringing new life and ideas to well-established organizations within the prolife movement.

Learn more at proloveministries.org

And Then
There Were None